Mapping Motivation

T0382955

Dedicated to
Linda E Sale, fine artist, fabulous wife, who motivates me
By giving me freedom and security and control,
Who enables me to create and learn and shine,
Who inspires me to compete and to belong,
And who helps me get the meaning.
What I mean is: she loves me.

Mapping Motivation

Unlocking the Key to Employee Energy and Engagement

JAMES SALE

Routledge
Taylor & Francis Group
LONDON AND NEW YORK

First published 2016 by Ashgate Publishing

2 Park Square, Milton Park, Abingdon, Oxon, OX14 4RN
605 Third Avenue, New York, NY 10017

Routledge is an imprint of the Taylor & Francis Group, an informa business

First issued in paperback 2020

Copyright © 2016 James Sale

James Sale has asserted his right under the Copyright, Designs and Patents Act, 1988, to be identified as the author of this work.

All rights reserved. No part of this book may be reprinted or reproduced or utilised in any form or by any electronic, mechanical, or other means, now known or hereafter invented, including photocopying and recording, or in any information storage or retrieval system, without permission in writing from the publishers.

Notice:
Product or corporate names may be trademarks or registered trademarks, and are used only for identification and explanation without intent to infringe.

British Library Cataloguing in Publication Data
A catalogue record for this book is available from the British Library

Library of Congress Cataloging-in-Publication Data
Sale, James.
  Mapping motivation : unlocking the key to employee energy and engagement / by James Sale.
    pages cm
  Includes bibliographical references and index.
  ISBN 978-1-4724-5927-5 (hardback : alk. paper)
  1. Employee motivation. 2. Employee morale. I. Title.
  HF5549.5.M63S235 2016
  658.3'14--dc23

                                                                    2015018107

  ISBN 978-1-4724-5927-5 (hbk)
  ISBN 978-0-367-78771-4 (pbk)

Contents

List of Figures

Acknowledgements

James Watson and Rob Breeds for contributions to Map design and implementation too profound to repay, and for their insight and ideas too. But for Rob (with Emma), we hope more Bakewell tart and pizzas are a step in the right direction!

The Ordnance Survey, and especially Andrew Loveless for his vision in seeing so deeply how Motivational Maps could add value; and Jayne Beresford, for her faultless execution of the programme and her invaluable assistance in providing the case study.

The John Lewis Partnership and Susannah Brade-Waring of Aspirin Business Solutions (and a Senior Practitioner of Motivational Maps) for a remarkable demonstration of their power, and the resulting case study.

Mark Turner and Steve Jones for being the earliest adapters and visionaries, and for holding the faith.

David Foster and Tim Bullock for invaluable advice and support from the beginning.

Keith Robson, who sustained us when we were flagging.

Victor Tardieu, a pre-eminent Map champion, and Craig McVoy too!

Anninna Davie, who gave excellent legal advice at the beginning and fabulous commitment; and Sue Kerr, who has always been there supporting us.

Steve Feltham – the quality guru par excellence – for getting Motivational Maps to the point where it could be successfully accredited: ISO 17065.

All my Senior Map Practitioners who drive this tool into organisations and make motivation happen: Akeela Davis, Alex Hicks, Jane Thomas, Roy Duffy, Sylvie Carter, Bevis Moynan, Lynne Bell, and Kate Turner; and all the Business and Licensed Map Practitioners who also make this *the* tool for making individual, team, and organisational differences.

SME clients especially who have loved this tool and worked so well with it: Philip Warr and Paula Warburton (PH Warr PLC), Ross Thornley (RT Media), John Davies (TDSi), Ben Marsh and Nic Canfor (Imeta), Penny Jepson (now JLT Specialty Limited), Simon Annicchiarico (Appius International), Clare Bell and Keeley Hemmings (Motorpoint); and the list goes on and on. You know who you are – thank you.

Jim Sweetman, Morag McGill, and Leslie Gardner for early feedback and support on the book project.

Professor Nigel MacLennan, a friend and thinker, who through his Advanced Leadership Conference introduced me to Gower Publishing.

Tony Henderson for his vision and enthusiasm for all things Maps.

Finally, Kristina Abbotts, a staggeringly brilliant editor and inspirer from Gower.

Preface

Dear Reader,

You may be asking, Why the title 'Mapping Motivation'? The word 'mapping' is such an evocative and powerful word: it suggests coverage and spread, practicality and usefulness, information and direction, exploration and revelation, precision and detail, and more besides. This book attempts to look at all these things: it covers what motivation is and how it spreads into virtually every aspect of our lives; it shows beyond question not only how practical and useful motivation is, but necessary too; it provides crucial information about the nine directions of motivation; it explores in depth its origins, its power, its relationships with key aspects of organisational management and reveals, amongst other things, new paradigms of engagement, team building and leadership development; and further still it delivers the precise language and the detailed metrics which mean that we can exactly describe motivations and measure them with acute accuracy.

This last point leads on to perhaps the single most important reason why anyone responsible for managing, leading, or consulting anybody else about people should be reading this book: it is because we can now have meaningful conversations not only about our own motivations (that is, our own interior and emotional landscapes) but about others' too, whether they be employees or managers. We can have non-judgemental, non-blaming, real conversations about how we feel and what we want without stumbling and groping around in the dark fog of our own false self-image and in the subtle quicksand of our own inappropriate languages. This is one of the amazing things about Motivational Maps – it reveals what most people do not really know about themselves. Our egos distort our sense of what we really want; and, anyway, we often end up wanting what other people say they want – e.g. money – just in order to fit in. The Maps cut across all this and reveal what we really want: what we want at a given moment in time. (As you will see in Chapter 2, motivations change over time because our beliefs do, and so this is a highly dynamic system.) Thus, Motivational Maps enables conversations where we can share our destinations through a common atlas of our emotional world.

This is a far cry from what I like to call 'Ra-Ra' motivation (artificially stimulating motivation through specific and often extreme events, e.g. fire-walking), or the basic notion that people either move away from pain or towards pleasure, which is true but of limited usefulness. Indeed, Motivational Maps invites you, as befits a map, on a journey of discovery in which you can become the authority on your own motivations and, moreover, can even become authoritative about them. Once you have done a Motivational Map you do not necessarily need an expert to tell you, although a qualified expert may well be able to add more depth to your understanding and insight. Furthermore, as you will discover, because your motivators change, there is no sense in which the language fixes or – to use a more pejorative term – stereotypes you. As your beliefs change, so your motivators also change, and so your motivational profile – your Map – alters accordingly to reflect what you really want. You can always have a 'bearing', then, on what you desire. This, surely, is a huge advance on where we are now: so many people not knowing what they want, confused about what they want to do, and frankly ignorant of the future they need to start creating for themselves. From my own perspective I just wish I could have done a Motivational Map when I was 18 and 25 and 35, and so could have jumped so many of the mistakes I made early in my career.

It is important to realise that all self-development begins with self-awareness; this is a quintessential tool for raising the quality of one's self-awareness; and the great thing, too, is that the Motivational Map does not stop there. Organisations aren't genuinely interested in increasing employee self-awareness. They want results: more performance and more productivity. Self-awareness can only be a feature for them of the benefit they seek. So Motivational Maps are expressly geared around not just raising self-awareness but also on providing what it calls 'Reward Strategies'. Put another way: knowing what I want in order to motivate myself, the best thing I can do is give it to myself – and that will energise me even more. And thus with employees: if we know what they want, and we arrange or rearrange our rewards and environment around those desires, and we satisfy them, then we are going to get some incredibly productive people working and contributing in our organisations. This is the promise; and for those who like their endings first, you may wish to take a peek at the two case studies in Chapter 9 to see substantial evidence of this.

The journey for me has been a voyage of discovery, and a voyage I had to make myself. Like all true voyages, all the knowns are not known before, and mostly they are discovered along the way. One of the most astonishing things about these discoveries is that they are not logical, sequential, or even really provable – except, most importantly, in the sense that they work. We may weary of the disputes between, say, Freudians and Jungians, but in so far as they are relevant today it is because they say something that is relevant to helping us solve today's issues – or, in other words, that they work!

But alongside my voyage of discovery, what qualifications do I have for writing this book? It's a fair question. My own background is literary and educational,[1] and not psychological or assessment orientated, and so I am from 'outside the field'. In a sense, too, I am an autodidact. So I take comfort from Professor Nigel MacLennan's observation – 'In short, superior performance almost certainly comes from self-taught performers'[2] – and from Peter Drucker's: 'Whenever anything is being accomplished, it is being done, I have learned, by a monomaniac with a mission.'[3]

I have been a monomaniac with a mission these last 10 years or so as I have struggled to understand motivation and to create a model that really works in the real world of organisational life. The Motivational Maps went live online at exactly the same time as the company, Motivational Maps, was incorporated in 2006. Since then over 20,000 Maps have been done; the questionnaire is in six (soon to be seven, as French is added) languages; the product operates in 13 countries; something approaching 500 organisations have used Maps; and there are over 100 consultants, coaches, and trainers who are qualified in its application. Recently, too, the Motivational Maps achieved International Organization for Standardization certification, ISO 17065, for the product.[4] The aforementioned case studies in Chapter 9 also highlight the credentials of this unique tool. But in a way all these statistics and facts are less than one simple principle that Bill J. Bonnstetter enunciated in his enthusiastic endorsement of the DISC psychometric, for he said: 'Its [DISC's] validity is proven just by watching people.'[5] Whether it is true for DISC or not I cannot say, as I am not an expert on that particular system; but I certainly can say this is true for Motivational Maps in the sense that for nine years now I have been staggered by the common theme running through feedback about the Map: 'uncannily accurate … spookily accurate … spot-on', and on and on.

People have recognised themselves fully drawn in the descriptions and pictures that the Maps draw of them. Incredibly, too, this happens whether the person being mapped believes in the product or not. We have had sceptics, cynics, employees seeking to disprove the Maps, and those who 'know' what motivates them beyond a shadow of doubt; and what have we found? We have found almost without exception these same people confessing that the Map is accurate and right and valid – that it is telling them something that they did not know before about themselves, and that what they thought before about themselves was inaccurate and incorrect.

Therefore, you are going to have an opportunity to complete a full Motivational Map as part of the course of reading this book. The relevant section of the book where you will find your opportunity to do this is in Chapter 4. Go there now if you need to and cannot wait.

Finally, creativity involves new insights and new ways of thinking, and this book is designed to give you just that. But with creativity goes innovation, which is about new ways of doing things. I want this new paradigm to produce just such action because at the end of the day motivation is about stimulating movement, is about motion. I hope once you have read this book you will be wiser and more knowledgeable about motivation; but, more than that, you will want to join the worldwide motivational revolution that is occurring via Motivational Maps: perhaps your organisation needs to consider how this astonishing product can help you in so many ways. Read on …

Notes

1   So what motivates this or that character, or this or that student, has always been a vital question for me.

2   Nigel MacLennan, *Coaching and Mentoring*. Aldershot: Gower, 1995.

3   Peter F. Drucker, *Adventures of a Bystander*. New York: Wiley, 1998.

4   Certification at http://www.irqao.org/PDF/C11364–31620.pdf.

5   Bill J. Bonnstetter et al., *The Universal Language DISC: A Reference Manual*. [Scottsdale, AZ]: Target Training International (TTI), 1993.

Introduction

It is undoubtedly the case that motivation is one of the most important topics in the world; but it is not generally considered as such. We clearly see its application to sport; we think it might be desirable in organisational life; and surely it would be 'nice', but not necessary, if we had some ourselves. And that's it. But, as Dr Raj Persaud wrote: 'Although motivation matters, it's difficult to measure scientifically. This explains why it has been neglected by behavioural scientists, when it might actually be the most important variable of all in human behaviour.'[1]

This book addresses the issue of motivation head on, and specifically the idea of measuring it; and indeed, before we even measure it, we need to describe it. Motivation is neglected because there is no language to describe it and no metric to measure it, and so it seems hopelessly impressionistic, wildly subjective, and entirely personal. We cannot, it appears, tweak or control the levers that enable this phenomenon to occur. Hence, in the real world, management's general distaste and avoidance of the topic in any serious format because they cannot answer this simple question: Where's the motivation spreadsheet?

Before we go any further, then, we might like to ask another question: Why are you reading this book?

Complete this sentence stem:

I am reading this book because …

Here are some possible answers. You want to be entertained. You want to be informed. You want to develop new skills. You want to help your career. You are curious. You want to increase the sense of your control. Or are there other reasons? In truth, you are reading this book because … you are motivated to do so. Why? Because you expect some benefit – and at the point at which you stop believing in that benefit your motivation to continue reading dries up. Motivation, as we are going to see, is intimately connected to our core beliefs; and these core beliefs affect every part and aspect of our lives. As David Langdon puts it; 'When you are motivated you have a clear sense of purpose, energy, perseverance and resilience. Demotivation is less defined and is often not something we are conscious of; it creeps up on us.'[2] The creeping up on us is perhaps the most disturbing factor of all; we scarcely are aware of our low motivation and the damage it can do, till finally we find: 'A breakdown in motivation not only becomes self-fulfilling, but can also lead to severe psychological problems, if it leads to hopelessness and the feeling that things are not going to get better in the future.'[3]

This book is primarily concerned with the operation of motivation in the workplace, in organisational life; but it should not be forgotten at any point that motivation is a life issue, a life quality issue, and that its absence has dire consequences for us at all levels of our life, not just at work. This being so, we are entering or engaging with a new paradigm here.

But it didn't start that way of course; it never does. It began as a simple discovery to help solve a constant and persistent problem that client after client identified: namely, what to do about motivating employees. Sure, there were loads of textbooks and handbooks that mentioned motivation; there were even academic theories and theorists extensively writing on the topic; and of course there are the ubiquitous motivational speakers who guarantee to motivate – well, at least for five minutes. But the reality is that the stranglehold of psychometrics has become too powerful and too pervasive. If something wasn't behaviour, then it wasn't real; and certainly it was not something that need concern organisations and businesses; only behaviours were … because they were, are 'sort of' measurable, and more importantly, yes, controllable; and that's what management wants: control!

With that in mind then it's easy to see why motivation is always the bridesmaid but never the bride. In *High Engagement*,[4] an otherwise excellent treatise on engagement, we find that engagement – the new buzz concept that will transform business – is part behaviour and part 'morale'. This is fine, except what is morale? How do we describe it? And equally important how do we measure it? But never mind that, so long as we have this strong behavioural component (of engagement) we feel we are being objective; we feel that we have a handle on the problem. Yes, we want engagement, but in reality are we simply going to end up with behavioural prods – sticks and carrots – that seem to work most of the time, or that replicate what that genius CEO at ABC Inc. did, and so that should work for us? In other words, will we have a tendency to do what has always been done, and address the external and visible behaviours, but do not penetrate into the inner and invisible sanctum: that place where motivation resides, where desire is, where what drives the behaviours makes its home? If so, then we ignore the causes and treat the symptoms.

So the paradigm shift is not just the idea that motivation is the missing core and essential component of engagement, and that motivation is a much better word than morale, but that organisations need to go way beyond behaviours in their dealings and management and leadership of employees, for behaviours are merely reflections, outward shows of deeper, invisible forces that are more effectively tackled inwardly rather than externally.

Before reflecting on this point, however, the question might be: why, again, is motivation a better word than morale? Essentially because motivation is a less nebulous, less intangible, less subjective a concept than morale; and this is even more the case since the advent of Motivational Maps, which has provided a descriptive language for the motivators of work as well as metrics that can measure them. Yes, motivation can be measured! Furthermore, 'morale' has a distinctively military connotation and association. It was most commonly used in the context of discussing the 'morale' of troops in wartime. So long, then, as organisations and companies remained wedded to a command and control model of leadership, this may not have been entirely inappropriate; but frankly, in today's egalitarian, democratic, fast-paced, and innovative environment there are 1,001 reasons (the most significant of which are discussed in this book) why command and control, except in exceptional (usually life or death) situations, is not the optimum way to compete in the modern world. On the contrary, bottom-up leadership trumps top-down almost every time.

This paradigm shift, then, has far-reaching implications: one being the impossibility of motivating employees with a top-down approach to management or leadership. To understand what motivates your employees and then to act on that understanding is to a. have a bottom-up approach, and b. to subordinate your needs to theirs. Incredible: to motivate or engage employees we need to *get* the idea that we achieve what we want through our employees getting what they want; thus, a primary aspect of any manager's job is ensuring that they understand what their employees actually want and take the steps that guarantee they get it. So a second and far-reaching implication of this work is that the role of the manager is subtly changing: it is not just about content, content, content – 'what are our goals, let's do it'. It is now about process: how do we get the people on board, so they want to do it? And this flags up a third point: the manager needs to be not exactly a professional psychologist but someone who really does seek to understand people. This then is less about the external world and more about the internal awareness, self-awareness, from which actions truly spring.

One of the most depressing things about presenting Motivational Maps to outmoded organisations with traditional managers – you know the types, I am sure: been there a long time, living on the capital and reputation of the past, self-important, know-it-all mentality, learning is a closed book – is the frequency and alacrity with which, on being told that the Maps will reveal the emotional landscape of their employees, they reply: 'I know my staff; there's nothing you can tell me about my men [or women].' (And yes, in case you are wondering, it's often the men saying this sort of thing.) Yet, if by some fluke they subsequently decide to complete the Motivational Map, they find that they were unable to predict their own motivators accurately; and given that, how do they imagine they could know what motivates their employees? So this is surely no surprise: to those who have more shall be given, and to those who have not, even what they think they have will be taken away.

We have, then, a revolutionary paradigm: instead of trying to manipulate behaviour, we are saying why not seek to understand the drivers – the motivators – themselves that each individual wants, and subsequently reward them on that basis? Let's do the same too for teams and whole organisations. To be even more direct: why not try it, for surely the results could not be worse than those we currently achieve with behavioural models? And to emphasise that point, what do I mean by worse than?

Three of the top research companies[5] in the world found respectively that only 31%, 21%, and 29% of employees were actively engaged, which means that the rest are either 'not engaged' or 'actively disengaged'. In other words, something like – without being too accurate about it[6] – 73% of employees are 'not engaged' or 'actively disengaged'; this is almost three-quarters of our employees. Add to this the observation that BlessingWhite repeatedly make – that 'The Engaged stay for what they can give, the Disengaged stay for what they can get'[7] – and we have a nightmare scenario and prospect for those organisations relying on the old models and management styles. We need engaged employees if we are to have any chance of our organisation becoming pre-eminent, of being valuable, or of being first in class or, better still, world class; and for engagement to occur we need to drive motivation into the workforce.

This book, then, is about helping you do just that. I'd like to think (although you the reader must be the judge) that this is a book crammed full of insights and ideas that can be used again and again to help motivate yourself and your employees. I'd like to think, too, that this is not a 30-page pamphlet that has been inflated by endless repetitions of a small number of suggestions into a stuffed and bilious tome. Instead, this work pays much re-reading and studying, although it is not academic; on the contrary, it is designed to be practical and helpful. For that reason there are notes and resources to give some support to readers who want more; but they are not given to 'prove' points or to justify positions and demonstrate arguments in an absolute sense, because 'the map is not the territory' and all models are approximations. The real issue is: which models are genuinely useful and productive? And so additionally, because this is not a theoretical work, many of the ideas in it almost verge on common sense; at least they do when you come to think of it. And I'd like to think that this is what I have done: I have come to think about it for a long time and these are some of my findings.

When G.K. Chesterton was criticised by a reader who spotted that Chesterton's comment that Charles Dickens' writings had been influenced by the caricature of English seaside postcards, and that this could not be true since such postcards had not been 'invented' till one year after Dickens' death, Chesterton's response was something like: 'A wonderful example of Dickens being ahead of his time'. I love that response, and leave you to anticipate how that might resonate with what we are covering here.

So, how should you use this book?

The book is divided into nine chapters plus a resources section at the end. It is best to read the book in sequence, as the knowledge is cumulative; and, given the fact the information and research presented on motivation and the nine types is entirely new, then it is important to grasp this model in order to understand all that follows it. That is not to say that specific areas cannot be dipped into if desired; once one has understood the core motivational principles outlined in the first four chapters, then one is freer to dip into the relationship of motivation with core management issues: performance, teams, appraisal, leadership, and engagement, in that order. Each chapter follows the same pattern: each topic is explored and this is interspersed with Activities and Figures. Again, there are usually about nine Activities per chapter; these range from a simple opportunity to reflect on the meaning of a word or concept or what it might mean to you, to more complex assignments which may produce real insights and deeper understandings of key principles and ideas. Of all the Activities the single most important is the opportunity in Chapter 4, Activity 5, to go online and generate your own Motivational Map. I strongly recommend you do this, and it is effectively the proof of the motivational pudding, as it were. Put another way, the Activities exist to help you interact with the book and its ideas, and to clarify and make them real for you. I believe that if you conscientiously follow through the Activities together with reading the text you will become an expert at motivation in a very practical and useful way. The Figures are there to illustrate some of the more advanced ideas, and often they include Tables documenting relevant data. Finally, each chapter ends with a nine-point summary that distils the essential learning points; these, along with the index at the end of the book, are a useful reference point.

The final chapter of the book, Chapter 9, is different from the others in that there are no Activities and no Summary. This is because the chapter presents two case studies of the Motivational Maps in two significant UK organisations: the Ordnance Survey and the John Lewis Partnership. Where possible I have left the wording of these case studies exactly as they were written by the two architects of the programmes, Jayne Beresford and Susannah Brade-Waring respectively, so that the reader can get a real sense of how this tool works and what kind of issues emerge and results occur. Clearly, if there were an Activity it would be this: what can you learn from these case studies to apply in your own organisations?

Finally, there is a Resources section. This is designed to supply links to Motivational Maps Ltd and its practitioners worldwide; other motivational resources and people; recommended books and information about motivation, and extended Figures that you may wish to duplicate and use. In short you have a mini-compendium of materials that will help you, especially if you are, or are seeking to be, involved with developing management or employee motivation; this could be for you as a coach, trainer, consultant, HR specialist, manager, organisational development expert, and so on. Dip in and enjoy!

Finally, I need to say that this book is really only an introduction to Mapping Motivation and there are several other major areas where it is being successfully applied, but which require more books to be written to cover them adequately. Briefly, then: Mapping Motivation can be used in recruitment, sales, management development, change management, and career development and choice. To touch on these areas one by one:

- Recruitment – motivation is an essential component of understanding whether or not a candidate is likely to be a high performer. The reason for this is very simple: the number one factor in hiring a successful candidate is that they have sustained levels of high energy. Motivation is energy, and so Mapping Motivations should be at the heart of recruitment.

- Sales – it is reckoned that at least 50% of any sale is a transfer of enthusiasm. All the sales technique in the world will falter before a prospect who senses that the seller has no enthusiasm for the sale or the product. As we discuss in Chapter 5, enthusiasm follows energy, which is again related to motivation.

- Management Development – depends on creating managers who have the skills and motivation to succeed in the twenty-first century. As we have said earlier in this very introduction, we need managers who are much more psychologically savvy, and specifically As we have said earlier in this very introduction, we need managers who are much more psychologically savvy, and specifically who understand their employees – the motivations of their employees!

- Change Management – is a dynamic process in which strategies and technologies and the market can shift almost overnight; if that is the case, then we need to understand the motivations of our people and to be able to motivate them to be able to cope, adapt, and thrive in all situations. In Chapter 6 we see how motivation is correlated with Speed, Risk, and Change – what could be more relevant?

- Career Development and Choice – it is important that we choose a career that motivates us. Simple? Yes, but not so obvious for most people. This is why there is a separate Youth Motivational Map – to help young people in schools and colleges make the right choices that fit what they are really looking for, instead of being 'safe' choices that they are going to hate later on.

I hope this brief introduction has whetted your appetite and that you are now raring to read on and explore the marvellous world of motivation. We welcome feedback, and you will find our details in the Resources section at the back of the book – do let us know what you think; and for the final time: make sure you do your Motivational Map. As a Hobbit once said, 'That's a real eye-opener for sure!'

Notes

[1]   Raj Persaud, *The Motivated Mind*. London: Bantam, 2005, p. 66.

2   David Langdon, director of business psychology company Xancam, and cited by Victoria Hoban, How to deal with a demotivated team, https://www.i-l-m.com/Insight/Edge/2013/May/dealing-with-demotivation, 24 April 2013.

3   Raj Persaud, *Staying Sane*. London: Bantam, 2011.

4   David Bowles and Cary L. Cooper, *The High Engagement Work Culture: Balancing Me and We*. Basingstoke: Palgrave Macmillan, 2012.

5   BlessingWhite, Towers Watson, and Gallup.

6   As it varies from year to year anyway, and also from country to country; also there are even gender differences.

7   BlessingWhite, *Employee Engagement Research Update*, 2013.

Chapter 1

What is Motivation?

Like most people, you probably feel that you know something about motivation. In exactly the same way people feel – because they can speak and write – they know something about language, or because they have been to school they know something about education. We see people who are motivated maybe on a daily basis, or we see newspapers or hear pundits in the media talking of sports heroes or heroines who are motivated. Thus motivation is all around us. According to Maehr and Meyer, 'Motivation is a word that is part of the popular culture as few other psychological concepts are.'[1] Having frequent experience of something can mean in our own mind that we are familiar with it, that we know it. We know 'something' about motivation, don't we, but what exactly?

ACTIVITY 1

Write one sentence in which you describe what you think motivation is. After you have done it, compare your view with the suggestions below. What do you learn from this?

Motivation is the motive – the internal reason – we have which prompts us to act in certain ways and directions. In a deep sense motivation is not a thought, since that would be purely intellectual. When we are motivated, whatever we are thinking is always hitched to an extra element that appears or feels electrical. Of course we cannot 'see' electricity; it is invisible; but we detect it from its powerful effects.

But if motivation is like electricity, it can flow both ways: its power and intensity can wax and wane; and although its effects are felt, it is itself, as we said, invisible. So the best parallel of all – and the one most frequently used in motivational literature – is with energy; the flow of energy within us. And this fits with the word's etymology – from the Anglo-Norman term 'motif', which is often translated as 'drive'. So, drive and energy are two powerful synonyms for motivation. But we need to remember that energy is energy; or, put another way, as Hilgard and Marquis put it:

> *The motivation of behavior comes about through the existence of conditions (drive-establishing operations) which release energy originating in the organism's metabolic processes. This energy, in and of itself, is directionless and may serve any of a variety of motivational objectives.*[2]

Thus motivation as energy per se is directionless – although of course what we will be interested in and what this book is about is energy at work and the nine directions in which it wishes to flow. But for now consider the importance of having energy at all: what happens to us, our teams, our organisations, our world, without energy?

The answer is: not a lot! Indeed, energy, and so motivation, can truly be said to correlate with the quality of our lives – not just at work, but also in our private and personal environments. One may have many disadvantages in life – a low IQ, a poor family background, a bad education, and so on – but having high, even very high, levels of energy is a massive compensation if only because (and it is not the only reason) having high levels of energy feels good. Indeed, it feels so good that all psychologically healthy people desire it. They are motivated to be motivated. In this way it becomes an immunity booster, a stress buster, almost an optimism barometer whatever else is going on. Truly, one has the energy to cope with difficulties, problems, and situations – and often to thrive in the midst of them.

ACTIVITY 2

What are the benefits of having high levels of energy, besides its feeling good?[3] Make a list and when you have done it, prioritise: what are the top three reasons why high energy – and so high motivation – is beneficial?

It should be clear, then, that everyone needs motivation, but whether they want it is another question. This may sound paradoxical, but it is true. On an even bigger level it might be argued that it is self-evident that everyone needs life – but strangely not everyone wants it. Yet, for all that (returning to the topic of energy and motivation), everywhere we look we see the need. People need motivation, and this issue becomes paramount when we consider employees within organisations.

If, for example, we turn to any classroom – and see the teacher who may have set out with the best intentions in the world to deliver a quality education to students. Now, bogged down by bureaucracy, guidelines, inspections, and procedures, lessons are delivered without relevance or enthusiasm. Energy – motivation – is ebbing away.

Or consider the students themselves: where a target-driven education bears little relationship to their reality, or to the deep springs of learning within each one of us. They too lack motivation, or at best merely have some desire for qualifications to enable their advancement to the next stage of the process. They achieve qualifications, but are they motivated to learn – especially to go on to that much-vaunted political credo: life-long learning?

There has been a lot of discussion on the new 'Generation Y' (those born from 1982 to 2001)[4] who are our future and who we need to be motivated. Some of their characteristics are alleged to be:

bored by routine

lifestyle centred

technically fluent

connected … 24/7

self-confident

success driven

anti-commitment

goal oriented

opinionated.

Clearly, education has to change if it is going to engage this generation. How do we sustain motivation with this group, given their characteristics?

Also, think about a Monday morning – classic heart attack time, or what might be termed the Optimal Work Aversion Moment. So many people are demotivated at the thought of having to go to work after the weekend that it generates more heart attacks than at any other time of the week. Indeed, German researchers found that the risk of a heart attack is 33 per cent higher on Monday than on any other day. Work itself is a word almost synonymous with the word *onerous*. Who wants to work? And this is despite the researcher Donald Hebb's findings that 'the human liking for work is not a rare phenomenon, but general.'[5] But how does that square with what we encounter on a near daily basis: namely, fewer people seem to like work and increasingly regard it as a chore; yet they need it and, sadly, most need to work.

Again, what we are talking about here is the quality of our lives. Independent of whether we have high IQs or low ones, whether we are tall or short, or even whether we are rich or poor, perhaps the biggest single determinant of the quality of our lives is how motivated we are at any given moment, and over prolonged periods of time.

ACTIVITY 3

Ask yourself the question: over the last six months how motivated have you been at work, in your personal life, in your relationships? Be specific. Score each arena out of 10 (10 being fully motivated/energised and 1 being completed demotivated/ de-energised). And how would you rate your overall motivation out of 10? Are you satisfied with the answer?

Why is motivation so correlated with the quality of our lives? Because, as we said before, motivation is virtually synonymous with the word energy – our motivation determines our energy level, generates our energy. And when we are fully motivated, we tend to be bursting with energy. When we are bursting with energy, then life feels good – stress has less power to touch us, and all our other problems are contextualised into manageable proportions. And one final extra point for now: 'feeling good' may sound somewhat 'hippy' and insubstantial, as if it were some luxury we could all do well without. But it turns out to be essential in many ways, the most important of which is our self-esteem, for our self-esteem fundamentally is about how much we like ourselves: the more you like yourself, the higher your levels of self-esteem. Clearly, the more you feel good about yourself, the more likely you are to like yourself. The importance of this will be clear in Chapter 2 when we discuss this in more detail, but for now all we need say is that high levels of self-esteem are essential to all areas of success in your life.

Thus it is that we need to pay attention to motivation – especially *our* motivation, and by extension to our motivators.

ACTIVITY 4

Ask yourself these three questions. First, how many hours per week do you spend on being physically fit? Second, how much time do you spend each week on promoting your health (for example, cooking your own meal, choosing healthy ingredients, as opposed to eating fast foods; or ensuring you get 7–8 hours' sleep each night, and so on)? Finally, how much time per week do you spend consciously motivating yourself? As you think about these questions, you might want to consider whether the time spent motivating yourself is enough, and in what it consists?

Here is a curious thing: many people spend time working their muscles and concentrating on physical fitness. Why? Because they understand that if they do not exercise their muscles they will wither. They will become, as people, impaired. This is fine physically, but what about psychologically? Two questions, then, arise: how do we know what our motivators are, and how do we stimulate our motivators?

One interesting thing about motivators is that they are closely allied to our values.[6] When we realise, or make manifest in our lives or the world, our values we become extremely happy or satisfied. So too with motivators – these are deep needs within us, and so deliberately feeding them in ourselves, or even attempting to feed them in someone else, is not 'manipulation' (how could it be?); rather, it is giving us or another person exactly what we want. And what we want is often more than what we need, or apart from what we need. Further, because motivation is intimately connected to our self-esteem, then it is also part of our performance matrix. And, finally, motivation is also part of our future, and our ability to realise that future. No motivation means no energy; and no energy means, at best, a deeply unsatisfying life.

ACTIVITY 5

Make a list of three things that motivate you at work. Try to keep the three things at a 'high generic level'. For example, going for a pizza every Friday with the team might be what motivates you, but that is extremely specific. At a high generic level this might be 'friendship' or 'belonging' or 'being sociable'. Or, if you wrote down that the excellent pension arrangements in your current job motivate you, what is the underlying motivator from that specific example? In this case it might be 'long-term security'.

Put them in rank order of priority. How do you know that your own rank order is correct, or even that you have identified your three top motivators?

ACTIVITY 5 (cont.)

Ask two or three people you know well and whom you trust to identify what they think are your top three motivators. Compare their answers with yours. From this establish what your top three most likely motivators ARE.

What then are the invisible motivators within us that drive and energise us to take action and adopt certain behaviours to pursue particular goals and desires? Each of us has the same nine motivators, present at all times; but the interesting thing is that they are in a different combination and order for each individual. For more information on why this is so, and the basis for this, see Chapter 3.

Figure 1.1   Nine motivators in 3×3 grid formation

There are nine motivators of work, and they are in a hierarchical order. Look at Figure 1.1. First, you will notice that they are in three groups of three; in other words, there are three main types of motivator – and in the case of work we might call them 'satisfactions' that we are looking for. The Relationship motivators we often think of as 'green' motivators; the 'Achievement' type motivators are 'red' and 'Growth' type motivators are 'blue'; and there is a lot more information about these three types and their important, indeed amazing, characteristics and properties, specifically as applicable to the work environment, in Chapter 6.

Second, however, notice that along with names for the three types of motivator we have given names to the nine motivators themselves. These are *our* names, and they are the best we could find that we felt were descriptive and yet brief enough to be useful. But here's the important point: it is this shared language that makes this such a powerful model. Using it, we can exactly describe – and so make 'visible' – the 'invisible' qualities of motivation. Remember what we said: we can't see electricity but we can certainly see or feel its effects. It is because there has been no real language to describe motivation before that the whole topic is largely avoided in business and organisational life. It's too nebulous a topic, too vague. This can now change: we have a language.

Third, you need now to familiarise yourself with this language and ask yourself again: what motivates you? Look at the descriptors in Figure 1.2.

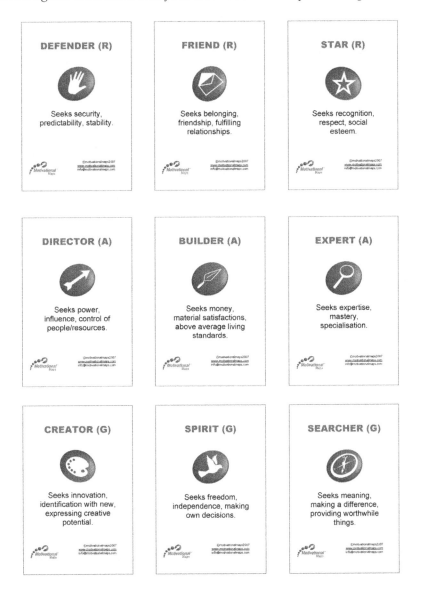

Figure 1.2   Rank order your motivators

ACTIVITY 6

Sort the nine motivators in order of their importance to you. Make a written record of your rank ordering of Figure 1.2.

- Does the overall profile match your current work role?
- How satisfied are you that the needs of your top three motivators are being met?
- What would you like to change?

Warning: It is highly likely that your view of your motivators is *incorrect*, that you do not indeed know yourself as well as you think you do. To find out what the actual rank order of your nine motivators is you will need to do the Motivational Map online. For more information and access go to Chapter 4 and Activity 5. When you have done it, why not compare this with your self-assessment?

- How accurate were you?
- Were you able to predict your three top motivators and in the correct order?
- If you manage others, what is the likelihood, if you cannot accurately predict your own motivators, that you could predict that of your employees or colleagues?
- What are the implications for productivity of not knowing your employees' motivators – their 'hot buttons', what turns them on, their energy source?

Clearly, at this point, if we don't know our employees' motivations and we are not addressing explicitly their motivational needs – or rather, their wants – then we are moving from the territory of discussing the dire outcomes of low motivation for the individual (and they seem serious enough as they impact quality of life) to the implications of low motivation, to the world of business and the organisational environment where thousands and sometimes tens of thousands of people are involved. What happens there? Is this just a 'quality of life' issue for them and the organisation?

ACTIVITY 7

Before reading ahead, list the consequences of poor employee motivation within an organisation. What do you think the worst consequence might be? And how serious is it?

Ultimately, with one proviso, organisations fail, and fail to survive even, if they ignore employee motivation over a prolonged and sustained period of time. All organisations that survive long term have loyal, engaged, and motivated workforces; they have to. The key words here are long term. And the proviso

What happens	Its Consequences
Employee Turnover – Up – employees leave	Costs £4.13bn per year UK across 5 sectors, £30K Per Person
Productivity – Down	Employees can be 16 Times Less Productive according to Pareto Principle
Absence Rates – Up – 'sickies'	Generates Low Morale, Low Energy, Low Self-Esteem
Recruitment Costs – Up – to replace lost & absent employees	Spent on Ads, Online Media, on Recruitment Agencies, and the Selection process itself
Fire-fighting – Up – as qualified and competent employees leave	Causes Stress and Health issues – so further absenteeism
Customers – Down – losing customers	Because Service is Poor, because employees they had a relationship with have gone
Reputation – Down – poor service and servicing the customer	This creates negative PR – typically one unhappy customer tells 13 others about their experience
Training Costs – Up to remedy the employee issues	But is the Training relevant? Tends to be Skills driven but motivation Is the issue – more waste of money?
Outsourcing Costs – Up – in order to compensate for insufficient employees, numerically and qualitatively	This becomes a Consultants' Paradise! Lots of fees paid to them!!!
Failure – Net Asset Value of the Organization goes Down	So Blame and Despair go Up – and we are in more danger of complete collapse

Figure 1.3   Low motivation within an organisation

is: yes, sure, short-term businesses and organisations – those exploiting the market or environment for a quick and easy buck, jumping on trends, jumping off again for another trend; those simply supplying basic commodities with no extra value – can survive short term with demotivated employees. But is that the way to go? Is that what we want for our organisations and businesses – short-termism and all its pain and despair?

Hardly! What we want are successful, creative, and motivated organisations that are adding value to their communities and to the world – organisations that effectively experience longevity as a result of their continual value-add. It needs to be said as well that individuals can perform at a high level with low motivation for a while, sometimes a long while; but this is always going against their own grain, and thus is highly stressful. Eventually it will lead to wasteful burnouts. So the question becomes: why is motivation often *not* in the workplace? If being motivated within an organisation is so self-evidently important for the long-term welfare of an organisation, then why is so little attention paid to it? Virtually all training and development is knowledge, skills, and competency based. This is an odd psychological reality which requires a detour.

ACTIVITY 8

Why do you think so little attention is paid to motivation within organisations? What could account for such neglect? And what would you recommend by way of countering this phenomenon?

I have already said that in most workplaces we find that most people are not highly motivated. Motivational Maps itself has had over 20,000 Map profiles completed with hundreds of organisations, and very few score in the higher motivation range. In many cases they are demotivated and even at a crisis point. People need to work, and their commitment to and engagement with their employer extends no further than the next pay cheque. This is not a desirable state of affairs, and there are many reasons for it; but perhaps the most unnoticed aspect of the whole business is how little attention employers pay to the issue. It's as if most of them live in a world where the motivation of employees – and of themselves (yes, of themselves too) – is the least important thing, and having the least impact of all on the bottom line. Unfortunately this assumption is wrong; but if we look deeper, matters are much worse.

The decision not to consider motivation as part of the business or organisational bottom line has profound psychological roots. It's not just that business owners, directors, and executives don't think about motivation – much – it's that they can't. This becomes clear when we look at the four major areas that underpin any business or organisation.

First, there is finance – the money. The Key Performance Indicators (KPIs) that drive the business are return on equity, profit, turnover, cash flow, and so on. When we think about these metrics, they are a yes–no or 1–0 situation: either we have the cash flow or turnover or relevant number (yes or 1), or we don't (no or 0). Accountants or financial directors, usually, supply us with this information. And when the worst occurs, and we have nothing in the kitty, we know that. In other words, for better or worse, we always know where we stand with the finance; we have certainty surrounding our knowledge of it, certainty even when the news is bad.

This principle also applies to the second area, sales and marketing, and also to the third: production and operations. Managers, for example, check on a daily, weekly, monthly, quarterly basis: how many leads, how many prospects, how many conversions, how many sales, and so how much revenue has been generated. Ditto for marketing: the advertising campaign, the web strategy, produces how many enquiries or clicks? And ditto for production: we ask how many widgets this month or how many service calls?

The point being that even when times are bad we know how we are doing. This is because we have Finance, Sales and Marketing, Operations directors, and managers keeping tabs on all this productivity and information through metrics. Metrics are critical because metrics enable measurement, and that is the foundation stone of us being able to perceive and know that we are making progress – or regressing – in our organisational work.

But, put another way, when we think about organisations, we have these types of directors in the main precisely because they attract the kind of people who are drawn to certainties: the spreadsheet full of numbers that tell us where we are. And if we invest in inputs we can measure the outputs, which are usually fairly predictable: for example, for every 100 leads that our marketing produces we convert about five on average into an actual sale.

Notice in this that whether the business or organisation is doing well or badly one thing remains constant in the three dominant areas of the organisation: namely, the psychological certainty of knowing where we are, of having the numbers which become our compass through the changing environment. This need for psychological certainty is compelling – it produces emotional security – but it has a disastrous side effect: in the fourth area – the people category (in which leadership, culture, morale, and motivation are included) – it doesn't work, for, as William Bruce Cameron put it: 'Not everything that counts can be counted, and not everything that can be counted counts.'[7]

| **Finance** – quantitative £ $ – ROE, ROI, profit, turnover, cash flow, etc

Psychological Certainty

No ambiguity about numbers

Comfort zone, less risky | **Marketing & Sales** – quantitative data – marketing mix, pricing, lead generation, clicks, conversion rates, etc

Psychological Certainty

No ambiguity about numbers

Comfort zone, less risky |
| **Operations** – quantitative data – productivity, levels of service, quality control, delivery capabilities, costs etc

Psychological Certainty

No ambiguity about numbers

Comfort zone, less risky | **People** – qualitative date – culture, leadership, commitment, motivation, engagement, values, etc

Psychological Uncertainty

Extreme ambiguity about meaning

Unpredictable zone, very risky |

Figure 1.4   Four key areas of organisations

Note: to be effective as an organisation, the four areas in Figure 1.4 need to interact and support each other. But also note, specifically, that in the area of people motivation, leadership, and culture we find that given inputs do not necessarily produce predictable outputs. The most frequent and outstanding example of this occurs with money: pay increases often demotivate employees despite the fact that a wage increase is precisely what they say they want. For example, everyone receives a 4% increase – which perhaps demotivates some employees who feel they have outperformed, but they have only received the same reward as everyone else; or they learn that a competitor organisation's employees all received a 6% rise. There is a well-known phenomenon in the stock market whereby traders can receive well in excess of £1 million as a bonus and yet feel aggrieved and underpaid!

The reasons for this are complex; but all MDs, CEOs, and executives will have stories not just of the failure of money to motivate, but the failure of dozens of other initiatives too: be they restructured flexi-time, increased time off, more training, better social events, environmental improvements, and so on. What would seem obviously a 'good thing' becomes for some reason a cause for disgruntlement. In short, the 'good thing' does not actually address what people really want, and usually this is because no one (no one in management that is) can be bothered to find out what that is. To be fair to managers, however: how could they do that?

ACTIVITY 9

Consider how, as a manager, you would establish what motivates your employees? How would you go about doing it? How would you be certain your assessment of their motivators was accurate? And if you accurately knew the motivators of your employees, what would you now do differently in terms of how you treat them? How much difference might that make – to their performance, their productivity, and to their satisfaction with work?

Thus in the people area or domain of organisational life, the certainties of numbers give way to uncertainty, and with that there are two corresponding phenomena: the rise of ambiguity, and the erosion of control. Most managers – exactly because they have sought to be managers – resent and resist these two tendencies. In fact the best way of dealing with them is by ignoring them altogether.

We 'contract' with people (don't we?) to do the work; we're paying them, so they should work, shouldn't they? A kind of blind-eye approach is adopted in principle, and only when things go seriously wrong – by which I mean the numbers all start going negative – is some attention paid to employee motivation – and usually, in a fairly simplistic way: let's send them on a course or fire them.

As a fascinating sidebar here, I would like to mention the concept of 'negative capability', which the poet John Keats long ago described as the quality that Shakespeare pre-eminently had, and which made him the genius he was. This negative capability was the condition in which one is 'capable of being in uncertainties, mysteries, doubts, without any irritable reaching after fact and reason'. Why should this be important? Because it sounds exactly like the condition we have been describing about how to deal with people, and it is reassuring to realise that it is also linked to deep creativity. So, though we are all prone to want facts and reasons for all that is occurring around us, ambiguity is important, and is at the heart of leadership, as it is of people. There is more on this in Chapter 8. But before returning to the main thrust of what we are describing, one further application of this concept might well be the issue of competencies. Competencies, in so far as they involve just ticking boxes, come nowhere near the qualities demanded of a leader; and, in fact, seem flatly to contradict the point that living with ambiguity is crucial. Perhaps, then, the tick box category 'Can live with ambiguity' can be abolished.

So back to the main thrust: what we have, then, are four areas of an organisation, three of which – Finance, Marketing and Sales, and Operations – produce emotional security in the way they are set up and designed to be measured. This means that directors and senior managers, by and large, have a massive disposition to want to deal with these areas *and*, correspondingly, subconsciously or otherwise, an aversion to actually dealing with the fourth and final area on which the other three really depend: the people.

At the end of the day all significant organisations depend on their people: their skill and knowledge; their loyalty, commitment, and engagement; their innovation and ideas; and their energy driving all these good things – their motivation. The Finance, the Marketing and Sales, and the Operations on their own, for all their certainties, can't produce a great or even a stable organisation; only people can – highly motivated people who are committed.

So managers and directors have to move away from their comfort zones and start more actively embracing the ambiguity that is people, and start making motivation a core organisational issue, even if the people area concerns itself with all that is not clear, measurable, and secure – indeed, concerns itself with all that is ambivalent and difficult to quantify. How are we going to do that? And what is it about people that makes them so intractable?

To answer the first question, this book is starting to take you on a journey in which we provide not only a language of motivation – the nine motivators that you have already encountered – but also some metrics. For the first time in organisational development we can confidently say that not only do we know exactly what motivates people, but also how motivated they are. This is an astonishing advance that this book is going to explain, demonstrate, and allow you to experience.

Second, regarding people's intractability, if we think about it, it is because life is really like that. Life is intractable. People are like life because people are life. To live is always to be aware of inherent difficulties (including death), whereas human civilisation and mankind's intellect tends to want to mask over these difficulties with its certain certainties, exact models, and clever constructions. In a way this masking over the ambiguities is natural enough since it enables people to focus on problems with a single lens, and this enables a lot to get done; yes, while at the same time ignoring what is inconvenient and troubling. At the organisational level this can mean, as an example, we are making massive profits while at the same time employees don't like us (the management). Never mind though, carry on making loads of money! Thus, profoundly, in dealing with the people area, 'management' is never enough: leadership is required, with all that that entails. Leaders – who motivate – are the only ones who can create real value; and that means embracing ambiguity.

Summary

1. Motivation is energy and has nine directions in which it likes to travel.

2. Motivation is critically important to and in our lives – it feels good.

3. We need to focus more on it as we would exercise or health.

4. Motivation is invariably correlated with the quality of our lives – with our energy levels, with our achievements, with our sense of satisfaction.

5. Identifying accurately your own motivators is no easy task.

6. The consequences for organisations of not paying attention to staff motivation are severe and ultimately terminal.

7. There are four major areas of organisational activity; motivation is core.

8. We have a new language and metric by which to describe and measure motivation.

9. We need better leadership, a leadership that embraces ambiguity and focuses on people and motivation.

ACTIVITY 10

List the three most important learning points for you from this chapter. Articulate how this has helped you think about either your life or your work. What three things might you do differently as a result of your new understanding?

Notes

[1]   Martin L. Maehr and Heather Meyer, Understanding motivation and schooling: Where we've been, where we are, and where we need to go, *Educational Psychology Review* 9/4 (1997): 371–409.

[2]   G.A. Kimble (ed.), *Hilgard and Marquis' Conditioning and Learning*, .New York: Appleton, 1961, p. 396.

[3]   For a more detailed discussion of the benefits of motivation see Chapter 5.

[4]   There is now post-2001 a Generation Z: all their qualities are yet to emerge, but some are said to be that they are 'digital natives', fully connected and communicating, plus valuing education, and even some 60% or so wanting to make a difference in the world. There are approximately 2 billion of them, so that could be a lot of difference.

[5]   D.O. Hebb, Drives and the C.N.S. (conceptual nervous system), *Psychological Review* 62/4 (1955): 243–54.

[6]   Our values are a form of belief: they are beliefs that we hold special or that we especially identify with and consider highly significant over other beliefs of lesser or contrary import.

[7]   William Bruce Cameron, *Informal Sociology: A Casual Introduction to Sociological Thinking*, New York: Random House, 1963.

Chapter 2

The Roots of Motivation

It should be clear from what has been said in Chapter 1 that motivation is essential if we are to achieve anything at work or in our lives, and furthermore if we are going to have a quality of life at all. But the question then arises: what are the sources of our motivation within us? Motivation causes us to act, but what causes the motivation itself? What are the roots of motivation?

There seems to be no clear academic agreement on this; various authorities cite different and differing models. For example, well-known theories include Ryan and Deci's Self-Determination Theory; Maslow's Hierarchy of Needs; Alderfer's ERG model, McClelland's Socially Acquired Needs; Herzberg's Motivator-Hygiene theory; and, most recently, E. Tory Higgins' Beyond Pleasure and Pain principles, which explain 'how motivation works'.[1] The important issue here is not to get lost in academic theories, but to realise that all models are approximations, are effectively metaphors, and that their value is precisely correlated to the degree to which they can help us understand motivation in a practical and real-world setting – organisational life as a case in point. In other words, their value is in their usefulness.

Given this requirement for usefulness and practicality, then understanding the roots of motivation will have real and positive implications for how we boost our motivation. To begin, it will mean that we can increasingly affect motivation, for what a useful model does is make the 'invisible' visible. Actions and behaviour are visible – we can clearly see them, but we do not see the motivations behind the action; instead, we infer them.

ACTIVITY 1

As a manager or coach of another person, why might inferring motivations be an issue? List some of the issues.[2]

Compare your behaviours or actions with your motivators – does one feed the other? Are there discrepancies – in other words, do you do things that are not

---

ACTIVITY 1 (cont.)

motivating for you? Why? What do you want to do that would be motivating that you currently do not do?

How clear are you about what motivates you? How sure are you that what you think are your motivators is accurate and really what you 'want'?

Of course, we may be right or wrong in our inferences. But what a model might do is give us specific information that helps us pinpoint what the real motivation is, and what it needs to sustain it. Motivation, we said earlier, and speaking metaphorically, is energy, a fuel that we are consuming; so what if our model enabled us to refuel ourselves?

My view is that there are three primary sources – or roots – of motivation within the human psyche. Two of the roots are 'malleable' to human 'thinking',[3] and so in some sense we can literally control our motivation; the other source or root is a 'given' and so is more fixed. (And at this point it is worth mentioning that this 'three' idea is quite thematic and recurrent, for three is a number that seems to press on and invade reality every way we look: the three dimensions of time, of space, of matter, and of much else.)

What, then, are the three elements of motivation within us?

ACTIVITY 2

Take a minute now to consider what you think are the three biggest sources of motivation within each one of us, in our psyche as it were. Why are we motivated, in other words?

I think the top three sources of motivation within each person are:

1. … .

2. … .

3. … .

Now compare your answers or thoughts with our suggestions. What do you learn from comparing these ideas?

The three primary sources of motivation are our:

• personality

- self-concept

- expectations.

Together they are like rivers which flow within us, and they stream into the turbulent sea or ocean of our fluctuating motivations. But unlike rivers, which are separate, they all interact with each other, and with the final outcome – our specific motivations in a given moment or period of time, continuously and continually.

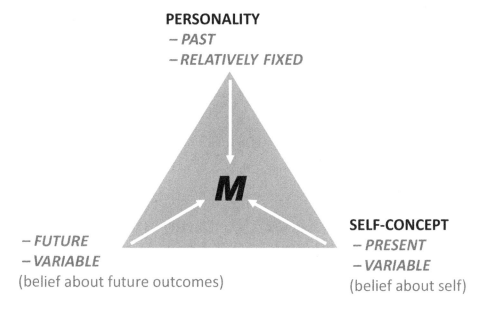

PERSONALITY
– PAST
– RELATIVELY FIXED

SELF-CONCEPT
– PRESENT
– VARIABLE
(belief about self)

– FUTURE
– VARIABLE
(belief about future outcomes)

Figure 2.1   Three sources of motivation in the human psyche

First is 'personality'. We are all familiar with the concept of our personality. In some ways it appears to be us; after all, it is our *person*-ality. There are various instruments – personality and psychometric tests – that measure 'personality', either our traits or types, or specifically the predictive behaviours which emerge from these traits or types. 'It' – the personality – appears to be relatively stable; personality can shift under pressure, but there seems to be a norm to which it reverts and wants to revert. In that sense, then, it appears to be a 'given'; our personality seems to be largely fixed and ordered at birth. I refer to this as 'past' tense: it goes back to our origin. That said, the fact the personality experts themselves consider increasingly that personality is malleable (indeed, that a person may appear to be very different at some future point in their life from what they were as, say, a younger person or as a pre-the-trauma person) only demonstrates the complexity of the human psyche and the fact that the self-concept and the expectations of an individual can, if prolonged or intense enough, have a profound effect on the personality.

The models of personality are various, and in the West seem to hinge on four basic types, which generate within them 16 subtypes.[4] Many organisations invest heavily in understanding the 16 subtypes of personality, but very few people seem to understand or rather 'get' the full range. The four basic types, on the other hand, are a different proposition.

In ancient times, for example in Greece or Elizabethan England, the four types were understood as representatives of the four Humours or the four Elements that composed matter. Classically, these were Earth, Air, Fire, and Water and they had properties very similar to the modern psychological types, only here we have dimensions such as extroversion v. introversion, logic v. emotion to categorise the type.

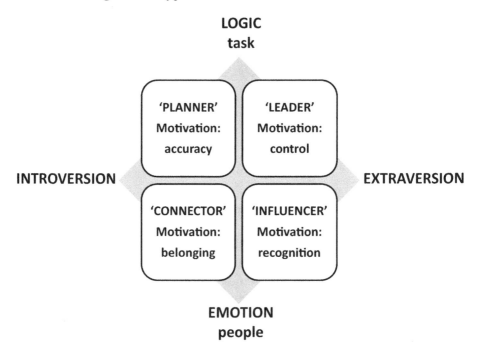

Figure 2.2   Four personality types

ACTIVITY 3

Where would you place yourself, personality-wise, on Figure 2.2?

Are you a Planner – getting it right, being accurate is your motivation? If so, you will tend to slower and more organised.

Are you a Leader – taking control, being in charge is your motivation? If so, you will tend to be faster and more organised.

Are you an Influencer – seeking recognition, wanting to be noticed is your motivation? If so, you will tend to be faster and more disorganised.

Are you a Connector – wanting to belong, forming strong relationships is your motivation? If so, you will tend to be slower and more disorganised.

Keep in mind that personal growth in this kind of model is said to come from strengthening your weaknesses by adopting the characteristics of your opposite personality type – that is, the one diagonally opposite you. If that is the case, then what are the implications for you of your type?

Within each personality type is a dominant 'hot button', which is a central desire/motivation of that type. For example in the 'Leader' type the motivational need is to 'control' – that is, if you will, the native motivator of that type.

You will notice from Figure 2.2 that the so-called Connector and Influencer types are in the emotional or people-oriented personality classification. On the other hand, Planner and Leader are in the logical or task-oriented classification.

If we superimpose this on the famous Maslow Hierarchy of Needs, the following interesting situation arises:

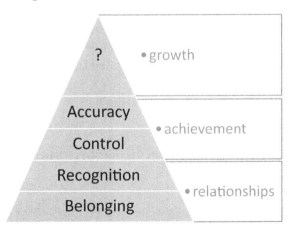

Figure 2.3   Maslow and personality motivation

The four personality motivators do not fall within the self-actualisation drives at the peak of the triangle. What this would appear to mean is: if our motivators are exactly what our personality profile suggests, then we would appear not to have done much personal development work – or, put another way, to have grown.

Remember, we said that the personality tends to be 'fixed' and past tense, which means that if that were all that was affecting our motivators, we would be static in our motivational attitudes. However, that is not what we experience in the world: motivation and motivators change. Why is this? One reason is that the sources of motivation within us have two other core roots – the self-concept and expectations – which re-enforce, overlay, or change the primary personality disposition. They also enable the 'higher' drives of the Maslow Hierarchy to be realised.

But before we look at these two variables, it is worth mentioning another model of personality that seems much more substantial than the standard Western four and 16 types. I refer to the Enneagram, perhaps the most fascinating and complex personality tool ever devised. The Enneagram goes back to the dawn of time, and certainly it was around at the time of Homer, usually considered to be about 800 BCE, although others claim it may be as early as 1200 BCE. The existence of the Enneagram is clear in Homer's *Odyssey* in that the perils that Odysseus faces are the nine personality types in reverse numerical order (Figure 2.4).[5]

In the Enneagram there are nine basic types of personality (although, like the four and 16 subdivision, the nine can be seen as 27 subtypes), each with their own qualities, motivations, virtues/strengths, and vices/weaknesses. Usually the nine types are identified by a number, 1–9. The nine types are also not entirely separated, but are divided into three blocks of three, according to whether they relate to the head, the heart, or the body.

Without going into this in further detail, the key things from our point of view are:

1.   All personalities are within the human psyche; it's not that we have 'one' personality and not the others.

2.   There are three basic groupings of personality: head, heart and body.

Type	Self-image	Defence mechanism	The Odyssey	Root problem
1	I am right	Control of reactions	Phaeacians of Scheria	Anger
2	I help	Repression	Calypso	Pride
3	I am successful	Identification	Scylla & Charybdis & Thrinakia	Deceit
4	I am different	Sublimation	Hades & Sirens	Envy
5	I see through	Withdrawal	Hermes & Circe	Avarice
6	I do my duty	Projection	Laestrygonia	Fear
7	I am happy	Rationalisation	Aeolia, Winds	Gluttony
8	I am strong	Denial	Cyclops	Lust
9	I am content	Numbing	Lotus-Eaters	Sloth

Figure 2.4   The Enneagram and the *Odyssey*

3.   One personality type is dominant but is influenced by its 'wings', subtypes, and connecting points, so each person has their own signature combination; one cannot change one's 'type'.

Clearly, from this it should be evident that this model and motivation are connected if not that they go hand in hand.

ACTIVITY 4

Look at Figure 2.5. Which is your Enneagram number or type?

Type	Self-image	Basic Desire (motivation)
1	I am right	To be good
2	I help	To feel love
3	I am successful	To feel valuable
4	I am different	To be unique
5	I see through	To master
6	I do my duty	To be supported
7	I am happy	To be satisfied
8	I am strong	To protect oneself
9	I am content	To experience wholeness

Figure 2.5   Enneagram type and self-image

Keep in mind when you consider which number most fits you that there is a strong probability that you will either be wrong (as most of us are not sufficiently self-aware) or that you will not know, because two or three of the number types appeal to you. That is normal. Also bear in mind that the Enneagram diagnostic tools can lead to conflicting answers: so subtle is our personality, so difficult sometimes to detect, and so easy for us to create a false self-image which disguises our real motivations even from ourselves. But given that you are correct, can you see how much of what you do in life is directed to fulfilling your Enneagram type? Like Motivational Maps, the Enneagram makes visible the invisible – our desires, our motivations, and, in the case of the Enneagram, our Self.

If personality, then, is the primary source of motivation, the second source is the self-concept; unlike personality, the self-concept is a much more fluid aspect of our psyche – less fixed, less innate, more 'variable'. The self-concept is how we see and feel about ourselves; ultimately, what we believe about ourselves and who we are. How we see our Self has an inordinate effect on what that Self becomes. For example, if we see our Self as being successful or content or attractive (or conversely substitute negative words) this will affect our motivation to do certain actions, to take more risks, and to develop the scope of what is possible. Research seems to indicate that the strength of the self-concept is a self-fulfilling prophecy – we become what we see ourselves as being.

Carl Rogers suggested that the self-concept has three different yet distinct components: the self-image, the self-esteem, and the ideal self.[6] In order then:

- The self-image is the view you have of yourself.

- The self-esteem is how much value you place on yourself, or more colloquially how much you like yourself.

- The ideal self is who you want to be or what you wish you were really like.

There is much that could be said of this model, but which takes us too far from the scope of this book presently; but two things must be commented on in passing. First, that this model of the self-concept is reflected in the structure of Motivational Maps too: the tripartite division for one thing, but alongside it is the time dimension, for if we think about it, the ideal self is very much future orientated, whereas the self-image is present orientated, and our feeling state, the self-esteem, is past; yet all interact and create one living self-concept in the present tense. We said something similar about Motivational Maps: each one of the three types of motivator – Relationship, Achievement, and Growth (RAG) – had an orientation towards the past or present or future. Second, to get a sense of just how important these ideas are to everyday life (since they may seem arcane), consider the words of William James concerning what we have described as the self-image: 'Whenever two people meet, there are really six people present. There is each man as he sees himself, each man as the other person sees him, and each man as he really is.' Isn't this spot on (apart, of course, from man meaning men *and* women)? Aren't we all aware in meeting others that what we see is not necessarily the reality that *is* that person, that self? We get to see something that is visible, but the true self may be invisible, and to know that is important because it will determine what actually happens in the real world.

With those points in mind, then, if we just consider the self-image, we have an important and dynamic link with the Enneagram personality tool: we have a view of our Self that we present to the world.

So, if personality is 'fixed' and past tense, then clearly the self-concept is effectively present tense – it's a view about ourselves now, which or may not be inordinately affected by past events and by *the* past (though one must say that the ideal self is of course a view of what we may wish to become, so there is a future component too). What this means from a motivational point of view is this: if our self-concept is bigger than our personality 'given', then our motivators will adjust to encompass that 'bigger-ness'. (And it needs to be said: if our self-concept shrinks, then a motivational sclerosis will kick in, and the range of activities we are motivated to do will diminish.)

ACTIVITY 5

Everyone has issues with their self-image from time to time – what we call a poor self-image. A poor self-image drains energy, leeches motivation, partly because our energy is spent on maintaining a false façade of who we are.

Figure 2.6 provides some stereotypes or caricatures of familiar poor self-images.

POOR SELF-IMAGES	
Narcissist	Mouse
Blamer	Perfectionist
Sarcasm	Addict
Comedian	Apologetic
Complainer	Gossip
Manipulator	First to the Bar
Sheep	Put-down expert
Big Mouth	Critic

Figure 2.6   Poor self-images

ACTIVITY 5 (cont.)

Do any of these ring true either in yourself (you as you are now or you in a younger incarnation) or in people you know? They may be slight tendencies or deep habitual modes of behaviour resulting from a poor self-image. Given these behaviours derive from poor self-images, then what beliefs feed, reinforce, and sustain them? Can you identify beliefs that have not served you well, that have impaired your energies and your life? What did you do about them? How can we – how can you – change our beliefs?

I have used the word 'see'; the self-concept, and especially the self-image component of it, is how we 'see' our Self. Perhaps a stronger and more accurate word would be 'believe' about our Self. Bear in mind the old adage: we do not see to believe, but we believe in order to see. Really the self-concept is our belief(s) internally directed; it is the fundamental beliefs about who we are, and so who we see we are. To the exact degree to which we can positively change our beliefs about our own internal representations, so to that same degree we can increase our motivation (amongst other important things).

Personality, then, is difficult to change and, indeed according to the Enneagram, may not really be changeable at all; but beliefs are – to some extent at least – changeable. This issue of belief leads on to the third root of motivation in the human psyche, and the second 'element' which is 'variable': namely, our expectations. Our expectations are – what?

Simply, expectations are our beliefs about future outcomes. Again, beliefs!

Before exploring this further, let us contrast our two 'variables' to get a sense of the difference and the similarity. If the expectations are our beliefs about future outcomes, then the self-concept, especially the self-image combined with the self-esteem, is our belief about our Self. Expectations, then, are beliefs mainly about results in the external world, whereas the self-image/esteem is a belief about our internal world, our Self. In essence both expectations and the self-image/esteem are beliefs directed outwardly and inwardly; beliefs affect our 'given' personality, and the beliefs determine all the outcomes of our life.

I think it is probably true that more people are inclined to develop (or not) their motivation via expectations rather than through developing their self-concept, although neither is a watertight compartment. The reason for this is obvious: once our attention is drawn to it our beliefs about future outcomes seem much more clearly linked to our energy than what we may believe about our 'Self', which might be considered wishy-washy or somewhat nebulous. (Of course nothing could actually be further from the truth.)

So, for example, if we had the opportunity to apply for a very prestigious and well-paid job, or to go on a date with an extremely attractive person, or to embark upon training for a major qualification, and we believed that the outcome of the job application, the date request, the likelihood of gaining the qualification was zero, how motivated would we be to start moving towards those desirable end results? Hardly at all for most people, and there would be every probability that we wouldn't even try.

At its extreme this opposite of positive expectation is called 'learned helplessness',[7] whereby the person expects nothing to turn out well, has no inclination to take control of their own life or to initiate action, and finally becomes co-dependent on others and/or entities (e.g. the state) in order to 'get by'. For these reasons even marketing clichés now advise 'Just Do It' or 'Can-Do' as a corrective to a lack of 'success' expectations.

By its very nature expectation has a future orientation: in essence expectations are beliefs about the future. So, the dynamics of motivation in the psyche are past-present-future orientated. The native root or base is our personality; but how we see our Self, or what we believe about our Self, interacts with the first root, as does our belief about future happenings and events. This, then, is a very dynamic model – any tool that could describe and measure motivation could only do so for an instant in time, because beliefs and so motivations will change over time. That said, of course, our core beliefs can be deeply entrenched, and it is also possible for our motivational profile to stay stable over long periods.

ACTIVITY 6

We all have expectations for the future, negative or positive. What are your expectations for your future? Do you expect things to turn out well or badly for you? Consider your expectations in the three main areas of RAG that we have identified. Over the next three months or three years or 30 years ask yourself:

How will my relationships (R) turn out? Think family and friends and others.

How will my career (A is achievement) turn out? Think work and income and success.

How will my personal development (G is growth) progress? Think learning and qualifications and expertise.

How do you think things will turn out for you? What beliefs do you think might cause you problems? What are you going to do about them?

Thus, it may be truly said – beyond motivation itself – that belief creates and makes reality for each and every one of us. We have within our own human make-up the power of belief which can change us, change the universe.

The implications, then, are tremendous. Over and above what might specifically be done to raise motivation via targeted 'reward strategy' interventions – which we touch on in Chapters 4, 5, and 8 – motivation can be increased by working on one's beliefs about oneself and about external reality itself.

Arvey et al. put job satisfaction (which is effectively motivational satisfaction) down to 70% environmental factors, and so only 30% to genetic influences.[8] These are approximate figures but it would seem reasonable, therefore, to assume that the personality probably accounts for about 30% of an individual's motivation, and the self-concept and their expectations the remaining 70%. This is a good working assumption to make (and not least because it means we are not determined wholly by our genes – a belief itself that has important ramifications),[9] but it needs also to be borne in mind that for some people these numbers will look wildly different. For example, the kind of person who has never engaged in any personal development or serious introspection, who has hardly been exposed to positive life experiences and success, is likely to be far more motivated by the raw components of their personality than by their developing self-concept and their advancing expectations. In such a situation the attitudes as well as the motivations of the individual are likely to be 'locked', or fixed, and they will experience change as threatening and difficult.

Such, then, is an overview of the sources of motivation within the human psyche. But if we are going to use motivation in the workplace and in life, we need a reliable tool, or diagnostic, that can describe, measure, monitor, and maximise motivation. Such a tool is the Motivational Map; because there are nine personalities with nine core motivators, it defines nine motivators and measures their respective intensities within each one of us. How is it constructed?

Given that motivation derives from three primary sources, then we need three inputs to provide data. For the personality the Enneagram provides a model and also two vital clues as to structure: there are nine core motivators and these nine motivators are 'related' in groups of three. For the self-concept we can use Maslow's Hierarchy of Needs which simultaneously describes human need, which becomes, as we ascend the pyramid, what we want – a kind of motivation – and at the same time a kind of progression. The progression is really from fatalism to freedom: at the level of survival needs individuals have no time to worry about what motivates them; indeed they are likely to ignore what motivates them in order to survive and get by.[10]

Finally, our expectations – our beliefs about future outcomes – can be represented by the well-known Career Anchors model devised by Edgar Schein. This is specifically future orientated because it is about linking our 'drives' with our career prospects – the jobs or roles in future which best suit our drives. 'Drives', like needs, is another synonym for motivation. Schein's original research found that there were eight drives that dictated what we wanted to work for. Subsequent reviews of his work in Israel by Danziger et al. supported his theory but held that there were nine drives, not eight.[11]

So we come back to this central idea that there are nine drives in Schein (future orientated) and nine personality types in the Enneagram (past orientated). These are models – 'maps' – not the territory; but it might be a reasonable assumption to suppose that there are nine distinctive motivators in the human psyche, and from this assumption we can start mapping what is happening with the internal energy we call motivation within each person.

If we attempt to superimpose the Enneagram, Career Anchors, and the Hierarchy of Needs (present orientation) into one model which also fits Motivational Maps, then we are clearly not going to get an exact fit; that would be too neat, and too unlike reality. But if we look at Figure 2.7 we do see, if we use an extended version of the Maslow Hierarchy which has eight categories of needs,[12] an astonishing set of parallel concepts across all four models.

So a central contention that we are going to explore in the next and succeeding chapters is that there are nine motivators in the human psyche; but unlike the Enneagram, which provides core and fixed elements of motivation, these motivators can change over time, just as our needs do on the Maslow Hierarchy. A change in our circumstances, in our situation, may mean a slow or a swift change in our beliefs: in our self-concept, beliefs directed inwards and about our Self; and in our expectations, beliefs directed outwardly and about outcomes.

ACTIVITY 7

Given that motivation and motivators for an individual change, what are the most important implications of this for you personally, for coaches and trainers, and for managers?

Make a list. What is the single most important implication? Why? And what actions do you need to consider in the light of it?[13]

Enneagram	Mot Maps			CAREER DRIVERS	MASLOW
				PURE CHALLENGE	BIOLOGICAL NEEDS
2	To feel love	**Friend**	to belong		BELONGINGNESS
3	To feel valuable	**Star**	to be recognised	LIFE STYLE	ESTEEM NEEDS
4	To be unique	**Creator**	to innovate	CREATIVITY	AESTHETIC NEEDS
5	To master	**Expert**	to master	TECHNICAL	COGNITIVE NEEDS
6	To be supported	**Defender**	to be secure	SECURITY	SAFETY NEEDS
7	To be satisfied	**Builder**	to possess more	ENTREPRENEURSHIP	ESTEEM NEEDS
8	To protect oneself	**Director**	to control	MANAGER	ESTEEM NEEDS
9	To experience wholeness	**Searcher**	to make a difference	SERVICE	TRANSCENDENCE
1	To be good	**Spirit**	to be free	AUTONOMY	SELF-ACTUALISATION

Figure 2.7   **Four models superimposed**

Motivational Maps, then, is derived from looking at core concepts within three models – the Enneagram, Edgar Schein's Career Anchors, and Maslow's Hierarchy of Needs – and seeing the overlay of ideas.

One final and vital point to make about Motivational Maps, which directly derives from its method of construction, is this: Motivational Maps is a non-stereotyping tool in its very nature. What do I mean by this, why is it so, and why is that important? To answer these points it is probably best to tell you a true story.

A friend of mine who was heavily and professionally involved in psychometric tools was at a party with his wife. She asked me, as she had heard a lot about Motivational Maps, whether she could do one, and I agreed to send her a code. After doing it she said, 'I love your Maps, love them.' Naturally, I was extremely pleased and after her effusion had died down, asked why. 'Because', she said, 'they don't stereotype me.' She then explained that the psychometrics that her husband used had categorised her as a Connector type – a helper, someone aware of the feelings of others, someone who wanted to belong. And

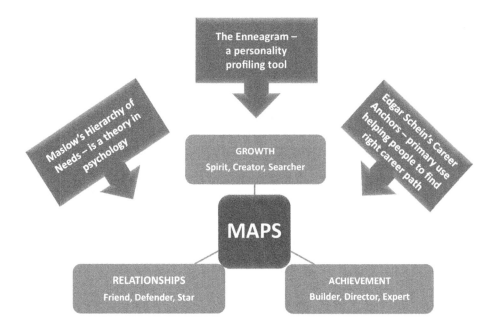

Figure 2.8   The models for Motivational Maps

this had 'fixed' how her husband perceived her; she was, therefore, almost by definition, not an ambitious person, or a leader, or a thinker. Her role was to support and help.

'But with your Maps', she said, 'I am a Creator. That makes me feel so good.' I smiled, but had to add: 'OK, but don't get too excited, because being a Creator isn't fixed forever and a day either. As you change, so will your motivators. That's the way it is.'

Still, she was very happy with this result and with the new self-image that it enabled her to cultivate. And if this seems a one-off, then think again. How many organisations appoint people on the basis of their psychometric 'fit' – on the basis of their fitting a stereotype – which they then want them to perpetuate? Very many indeed, and it is costing them a fortune.

An egregious example of this occurred in the UK recently with the revelation that the disgraced chairman of a bank had virtually been appointed to the post because of his psychometric results. The UK Government Treasury Committee, investigating the catastrophe and losses enveloping the bank as a result of the poor leadership, said of the disgraced chairman that he proved to be 'psychologically unbalanced but psychometrically brilliant'. The point here is that the stereotyping provided by the psychometric created the illusion of competence and 'fit', and once created nobody questioned either his competence or his suitability for the role till it was too late to challenge it.

Motivational Maps circumvent this problem – what I like to call the problem of the static (that is, you are static: the personality or psychometric tool largely fixes who you are rather like a fly is fixed in amber) – by assuming at the outset that your motivations will change. True, there is generally some stability for a period of time, but certainly within a two-year span there will be some shifts in your motivational profile. In other words, Motivational Maps is a dynamic model, changing as you change.

ACTIVITY 8

In Chapter 1, Activity 6, you attempted to rank order your top motivators as they are now. Think back five or 10 or 15 years in your life. Have your motivators changed? What do you think the rank order of your top three motivators were five, 10 and 15 years ago?

Top 3 Motivators Now	Top 3 Motivators 5 years ago	Top 3 Motivators 10 years ago	Top 3 Motivators 15 years ago

Figure 2.9   Reviewing past motivators

What do you learn about yourself as you consider these changes? What do you think may motivate you in future? Why?

Summary

1.   There are three roots of motivation in the human psyche.

2.   Personality, the first root, tends to be innate and fixed and past orientated.

3.   Whilst there are many 4 by 16 models of personality, the ancient Enneagram presents a compelling nine-type model.

4.   The self-concept and our expectations are the second and third roots of motivation, and they are present and future orientated – they change over time.

5.   Thus motivation changes over time.

6.   Approximately 70% of our motivation is determined by the self-concept and our expectation; in other words, by our beliefs.

7.   Three powerful and overlapping models that depict aspects of our personality, self-concept, and expectations are respectively, the Enneagram, Maslow's Hierarchy of Needs, and Edgar Schein's Career Anchors.

8.   Motivational Maps has been constructed from these three models.

9.   Motivational Maps do not stereotype people; indeed, they reflect how they change; the model is dynamic.

Notes

1   E. Tory Higgins, *Beyond Pleasure and Pain: How Motivation Works*, Oxford: Oxford University Press, 2014.

2   There can be many issues, but one is clearly that people intentionally or otherwise conceal their true motivations. A second is viewer bias or intentional distortion, in that we project onto others motivators we value in or of our self. Third is the issue we talked of earlier, namely, the lack of a sufficient language in which to describe our own, let alone another's, motivators.

3   Or, more precisely, 'belief', as we will see.

4   The most famous and well known is probably Myers-Briggs; others include DISC, Insights, 16PF, etc.

5   Michael J Goldberg (Goldberg Consulting), *Travels with Odysseus*, Tempe, AZ: Circe's Island, 2006; also see Judith Searle, *The Literary Enneagram*, Santa Monica: Ignudo, 2011.

6   Carl Rogers, A theory of therapy, personality and interpersonal relationships as developed in the client-centered framework. In S. Koch (ed.), *Psychology: A Study of a Science. Vol. 3: Formulations of the Person and the Social Context*, New York: McGraw-Hill, 1959.

[7] A term first coined by Martin Seligmann, *Learned Optimism*, New York: Vintage, 2006 (first published 1990).

[8] Arvey, R.D., T.J. Bouchard, N.L. Segal, and L.M. Abraham, Job satisfaction: Environmental and genetic components, *Journal of Applied Psychology* 74/2 (1989): 187–92: 'While the results indicate the majority of the variance in job satisfaction was due to environmental factors (70%), genetic influence is still a minor factor.'

[9] It allows for free will and so for personal responsibility; the alternative, that we are predestined by our genes (or fate or anything else), invariably leads to political extremism and to an erosion of our sense of the value of life.

[10] The implication of this, then, is that there is a small minority of people for whom the Motivational Map is accurate but irrelevant, since their 'needs' override their genuine motivators.

[11] Nira Danziger, Dalia Rachman-Moore, and Rony Valency, The construct validity of Schein's career anchors orientation inventory, *Career Development International* 13/1 (2008): 7–19: 'The study's contributions are threefold: first, it generally supports Schein's Career Anchor Theory, yet with nine anchors rather than with the original eight.' Also, see Dave Francis, *Managing Your Own Career* (London: Fontana, 1985), where he cites the Richmond study as identifying nine drivers.

[12] There are many versions of Maslow's Hierarchy, and not just by Maslow himself. See, for example, Alan Chapman's work on the Maslow Hierarchy at http://www.businessballs.com.

[13] The single most important implication of changing motivators is the need to review one's own motivational profile and the profile of employees regularly, for not to do this is to be potentially demotivating employees.

Chapter 3
The Nine Motivators and Their Properties

We have established that there are nine motivators in the human psyche, all of them always there, but in different combinations and intensities for different people because people have different but stable personalities (their Enneagram number and influences), different and complex self-concepts, and different and widely divergent expectations.

ACTIVITY I

There are nine motivators in the human psyche and each person can have them in any order; indeed over 20,000 Motivational Maps have been completed, and there are striking divergences in the rank ordering. How many possible combinations do you think there might be? And why might having a large number of possible combinations be a good thing? Are there any drawbacks?

Before looking at the nature and the definitions of these nine motivators it is useful to review just how many possible combinations there are. If there are nine motivators then the possible number of combinations is 9! – or $9 \times 8 \times 7 \times 6 \times 5 \times 4 \times 3 \times 2 \times 1 = 362,880$ combinations. If we then argue that the scoring range itself produces a minimum (although more in reality) of three clear levels (high, medium, and low) for each motivator, then the total number of possible combinations is $3 \times 362,880 = 1,088,640$. In short, Motivational Maps suggests that there are a minimum of 1 million clearly distinctive profiles possible with its model. With some 7 billion people on the planet this seems more realistic than, say, 12 for astrology or 16 for most psychometrics.

The nine motivators are shown in Figure 3.1 overleaf, which we briefly saw in Chapter 1. Now study these carefully to get a feel for what they represent.

Figure 3.1   Nine motivators in 3×3 grid formation

What, then, is the language of motivation that allows us to begin mapping it? Beginning at the base of the Maslow Hierarchy we start with the desire (or the want, or the energy) for security, or what we call the Defender. You will see from Figure 3.1 that security, the Defender, is the first of the three relationship motivators. We like to think of them as 'green' for foundational and root.

The Defender wants security, the Friend belonging, and the Star recognition; and what this means can be seen in Figure 3.2.

DEFENDER	FRIEND	STAR
High job security	Feeling of belonging	Social & public recognition
Clear roles and responsibilities	Nourishing & fulfilling relationships	Being noticed & held in high esteem
Regular and accurate information	Collaborative environment	Awards & certificates
Continuity and loyalty	Being liked & supported	Clear hierarchy / pecking order
Order and clarity	Being listened to	Competitive opportunities
Time to prepare	Loyalty & continuity	Positive feedback

Figure 3.2   Three relationship motivators and their values

ACTIVITY 2

Given their respective drives or wants, what kind of roles or situations do you think would suit the Defender, the Friend, and the Star? Treat each one in isolation, as if it were the only motivator in a person's profile. Go to Figure R.2 in the Resources section of this book for more information.

We should have little difficulty in understanding why we have called the Friend and the Star 'Relationship' motivators. Clearly, wanting to belong involves relationships with others, and equally clearly the desire for recognition presupposes other people who can supply it. But I am often asked how the root motivator – the Defender, the need for security – is a Relationship motivator. The answer is as surprising as it is compelling.

ACTIVITY 3

How do you think the desire for security, for predictability, and stability is a relationship issue? What's the connection between security and relationships? List some of the issues. How important a motivator is this? How strong do you think this desire is?

The truth is that human beings do not start life as adults, but as little babies, and in that condition they cannot 'achieve' security or very much else: they cannot feed, clean, or protect themselves. What they learn implicitly for the first two years of their life is that security – living itself – depends on another, the carer or parent who looks after and hopefully loves the infant. Thus security depends on the relationship with the parent, and it is impossible to shake off this learning, although many attempt to do so, thinking that what they achieve in later life will render them 'secure'. If they have enough power (Director) or enough money (Builder), or enough expertise and knowledge (Expert) they can by-pass the need for meaningful relationships with others. A great fictional example of this is the well-known Dr Gregory House, played by Hugh Laurie in the TV series *House*. He seems to think that his expertise in saving lives justifies his hostility to meaningful relationships; and clearly the success of the eight series meant that the public identified with this type of person. But all attempts to do this lead to a divorce from reality and the paradox that one ends up more vulnerable, more insecure, and more likely to fail.

This applies as much at a national level as it does individually: peace and security always come from constructive engagement and relationships with other countries, but not from a position of power, wealth, and superior technology. Indeed the reliance on power, wealth, and superior technology to manage one's relationships with others inevitably leads to resentment and a competitive desire to get 'even', or surpass, by those who feel oppressed by such power. Keep in mind that if this applies at a national level, then it will certainly also apply at the team and organisational level where motivation also operates in a highly significant way, as we will see in Chapters 6 and 8.

We start, then, with Maslow at the root of our need or want, and what I am calling the Relationship motivators. However, we need to be clear on one thing: all the motivators are equal and human, even though I have indicated that there is some sense of personal growth, as Maslow envisaged, in ascending the pyramid. Maslow's model has been criticised on several grounds, one being that important motivators like money or material prosperity are not included, although they appear fundamental. Perhaps from my perspective a more important critique would be to take his idea of D- and B-needs and reframe it.

Maslow thought that once our D-needs (or Deficiency) were met, we could go on to realise our B-needs (or Being); these latter needs were seen by him as growth needs. But in the West and in cultures and countries where basic physiological needs are met, where does the need end and the want begin? My position would be that they end quite quickly after the physiological needs are met, and then we don't just need but want 'things'. We want them more strongly because we feel entitled to have them.

Thus, we discount[1] the level of physiological need from the Mapping process because that truly is and can only be a need and not a motivator in the work-sense; and so I regard the need for security as the starting point of what we want, which I think it also is. This brings us back to the point about the motivators all being equal, for while growth is possible and desirable, all of us can revert back to 'lower' motivators given the relevant internal or external stimulation – in other words, via changes in our self-concept or in our expectations. This being the case, then, it is a necessary part of our survival mechanisms: we are unlikely to remain in a state of pure self-actualisation. On the contrary, suppose that our top three motivators are the three 'blue' or Growth motivators – Searcher, Spirit, and Creator – and have been for a while; and then catastrophe happens: we lose our job, our stocks and shares prove worthless, our partner leaves us abruptly, or there is the death of a close family member ... then maybe our motivators change, and change in an instant. Maybe we revert to the lowest motivators of all in the psychological index of wants: we want some security now (Defender) or we want to belong (Friend). Are these needs or are these wants? The question is almost academic, for whatever they are, they become the drives that may enable us to re-ascend the pyramid at some future time; they propel us forward, and so we can classify them as drives or wants without arguing needlessly over semantics.

ACTIVITY 4

What distinctions between needs and wants would you make? How do you see your motivators – as needs or wants? What difference to you or your decision-making process might such distinctions make?

An adapted Maslow's Hierarchy of Needs, then, pitted against the Motivational Maps, might look like Figure 3.3.

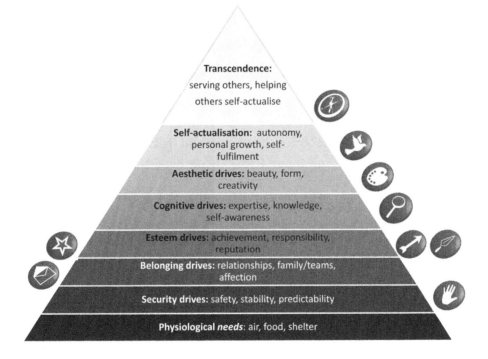

Figure 3.3   The Maslow Hierarchy and Motivational Map alignment

The nine motivators start at the base of the Maslow Hierarchy and work up to the peak. Next there are the three Achievement-type motivators: Director, Builder, and Expert. We like to think of them as 'red' for action and results.

The Director wants control, the Builder wants money, and the Expert wants expertise; and what this means can be seen in Figure 3.4.

DIRECTOR	BUILDER	EXPERT
Being in control / in charge	Above average standard of living	Opportunities to learn
Being stretched	Material and financial rewards	Specialising in areas of interest
Making critical decisions	Clear goals & targets	Opportunities to share expertise
Clearly defined career path	Work that is visibly well rewarded	Realising own potential
Having control of resources	Responsibility	Contact with other experts
Responsibility & influence	Competitive/targeted environment	Mastering their own work

Figure 3.4   Three Achievement motivators and their values

ACTIVITY 5

Given their respective drives or wants, what kind of roles or situations do you think would suit the Director, the Builder, and the Expert? Treat each one in isolation, as if it were the only motivator in a person's profile. Go to Figure R.2 in the Resources section of this book for more information.

It should be pretty obvious why these are called the Achievement motivators: they involve the basic activities that people within organisations and businesses undertake.

ACTIVITY 6

What are the three primary activities of people working in organisations? List them.

If we leave aside the activities that are more high level – strategy, marketing, and so forth – and focus on what is going on within, we find that organisations need to have managers (and ideally leaders too); and that they need to sell their products and services (and so have a competitive orientation); and finally, as part of both product and service development – as well as the sales process and the support systems – they need deep levels of expertise.

Thus fundamental work activities are driven by the Director motivator – to manage; the Builder motivator – to compete and make money; and the Expert motivator – to develop and exhibit advanced knowledge and skills. But it would be a mistake to think that only recruiting people with these motivators might make the perfect business combo.

ACTIVITY 7

What might be some of the problems with only having employees who were motivated only by control, or money, or expertise?[2]

Finally, in our triad of motivators, as we reach the pinnacle of the Maslow Hierarchy, we find the Growth motivators. We like to think of them of 'blue' for aspirational and upwards.

The Creator wants innovation, the Spirit wants autonomy, and the Searcher wants to make a difference; and what this means can be seen in Figure 3.5.

CREATOR	SPIRIT	SEARCHER
Environment with change & variety	Working autonomously	Meaning & purpose in what they do
Opportunity to solve problems	Making own decisions	Significant & important work
Being original	Having a choice	Making a difference
Creating something new/improved	Freedom & independence	Seeing the big picture
Ability to work alone / small groups	Awareness of the bigger picture	Being listened to / consulted
Recognition of their creativity	Clear & specific objectives	Change & variety

Figure 3.5   Three Growth motivators and their values

It is important to stress again that all motivators are good and equal; there is no such thing as a 'bad' motivational profile. There is only context: some profiles are more relevant to specific roles or situations. But motivators are not skills or knowledge. It is entirely possible for an individual to perform at a high level (because they have the appropriate skills and knowledge) yet be unmotivated. Entirely possible – but highly undesirable and ultimately unsustainable, for eventually to work at something that does not motivate you will drain your energy and lead to burnout or worse. To work at something that is not motivating for a prolonged period of time is stressful, so there will be health issues. And, quite apart from that, it is axiomatic that working at something that does motivate you is beneficial in every way: the performance will be higher still; the retention rate for the organisation will improve; teamwork will benefit; and that general sense of happiness or satisfaction at work will also increase. What's not to like about motivation?

ACTIVITY 8

Given their respective drives or wants, what kind of roles or situations do you think would suit the Creator, the Spirit, and the Searcher? Treat each one in isolation, as if it were the only motivator in a person's profile. Go to Figure R.2 in the Resources section of this book for more information.

We now need to examine more closely these three categories of motivation: Relationship, Achievement, and Growth. What else do we know about them? How do we achieve balance with them? And, specifically, what other properties do they have?

People today talk of the Work–Life Balance, which is good, but not entirely accurate. It suggests a split between work and life, and a choice between the two which can be remedied by information or techniques that will enable them to co-exist in harmony: you can have work and life. However, work is part of life and the split is not two ways, but three; and it is the invisible 'third' element that makes all the difference in practice to the other two.

When we think about it, for all our lives there are three core elements:

1.   There is work, in which we struggle to achieve something or impose our signature on the external environment.

2.   There is a relationship, or are relationships, in which we yearn to love and be loved by others, and gain their respect and co-operation.

3.   And, finally, there is self – our self, our real self – in which we seek
        to grow through self-awareness and self-development, and this
        imposes some sort of order and growth on our internal environment.

These elements are dynamically interacting all the time. The most obvious
example of this is when a colleague at work, known for their commitment
and skills and quality output, suddenly loses interest in what they are doing,
or becomes positively obstructive. Nobody can understand why this has
happened, but upon investigation the root problem turns out to be nothing to
do with work – turns out to be, for example, that their partner has left them or
a parent has suddenly died. Thus, relationships outside work affect the work.

If this is true, as most obviously it is, then it makes sense that the self,
too, will also affect both work and relationships, as work and relationships
affect the self. The problem is: very few people seem to understand that they
have a 'self' and that therefore they need to tend it. Tend it as you would a
garden, for in this way 'flowers' can grow – and Growth is possible. (It was
James Allen who made the observation that flowers needed cultivating in the
mind but weeds would and could grow in any case and without intervention.)[3]
The exception to this general stricture would be the physical self and physical
health. Because they can see and feel their physical bodies, people will take
action to promote its well-being, development, and growth; so they join the
gym, do yoga, eat well, and so on. Far fewer pay attention to their mental self,
their emotional self, and their spiritual self. This is a tragedy because it is the
self that primarily fuels work and relationships, as we shall see. It is this self
that seeks, in Maslow's terminology, to self-actualise or reach its potential; in
short, it seeks Growth.

However, before we discuss this in more detail, let's briefly look at how the
three life elements express themselves in our lives. If we were to sum up their
content in one question, then it would be:

- The Relationship element asks: how do I get strokes?[4] Three good
  examples of 'strokes' would be: how do I get approval, recognition,
  or appreciation?

- The Achievement (or Work) element asks: what do I do? How do I
  leave my mark in this world?

- And the Growth (or Self) element asks: what does this mean?
  Or, why am I doing this?

ACTIVITY 9

Ask yourself these three elemental questions. How do I get strokes when I am in any situation with others? What do I do in the world that makes my mark appear? And what does my life and experiences really mean? Spend some time reflecting on these questions and perhaps jot down your answers. You may wish to revisit them at some future time.

Notice that the Growth question answers the 'why' and, as has often been observed, human beings with a big enough 'why' have the energy to do anything and everything. Thus there are three types of motivator and it is their dynamic interaction that can provide us with the energy to go on, to refresh and replenish us.

All three questions are vital to us as human beings, but it should be clear that if we consider anybody, including our self, then we all have predilections. Some people regard the question 'what do I do?' as far more important than the other two. And what we observe is how this manifests itself in the world: in fact this question is particularly pertinent to men and can lead to the often observed work–life imbalance that is so characteristic of them. A form of workaholic-ism emerges whereby work becomes the be all and end all of their existence – and of course of some women's too.

Again, some people, and probably proportionally more women than men, regard the question of how I get strokes round here as the core issue of their lives. Relationships are everything, and in a way they are right. There is a familiar adage, 'all for love', and another which says that nobody on their deathbed wishes they had spent more time in the office. No, they wish they'd spent more time with the people they allegedly loved. But for all the power of love, the need for strokes can lead to compliance, co-dependence, and a loss of personal identity in the mad desire to have strokes come what may.

Finally, then, the third question, which seems cerebral and academic but upon which so much depends: what does this mean? In his book *Man's Search for Meaning* the noted psychologist Viktor Frankl concluded that the meaning question was at the core of our existence.[5] Man simply could not live without it, but with it could endure almost anything. This is fine and philosophical, but so many individuals are too busy to pay any attention to the question, and so to themselves, until it is too late. They mistake the customs, habits, and values of civilisation as a given font of meaning, and then do not have the internal equipment to deal with pressure when the cracks appear, as they always do to a greater or lesser extent.

So, to return to an earlier point, it is knowing the self, it is allowing for personal growth, that is the key to both success at work and in relationships; hence the Greek adage, sometimes referred to as Apollo's maxim, to increase self-awareness by 'knowing oneself'.[6] Further, it is the fuel that provides the 'energy', or motivation if you will, to these other two elements. Ultimately, the person who is either so busy working or so busy in a relationship (say, caring for a child), or both, burns out because there is no 'time for myself'. Time for the self is critical, but using it wisely is a different matter, for it is in those spaces between the work and the relationships that many find being on their own, with their self, unbearable – and so need narcotics, stimulants, or entertainment of one sort or another to cope. As Pascal, perhaps rhetorically, put it: 'All man's evil comes from a single cause, his inability to sit still in a room.'

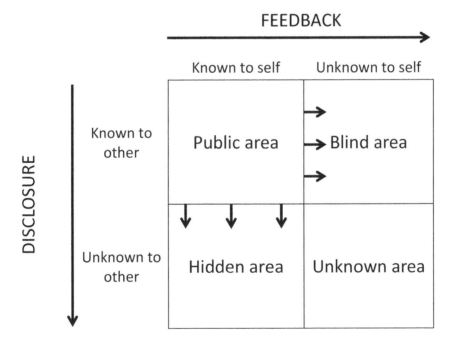

Figure 3.6   Feedback and the Johari Window

Study Figure 3.6 and you will see that there are four possibilities about self-awareness: things you know about yourself and others do (public area); things you know about yourself but others don't (hidden area); things you don't know about yourself and neither do others (unknown area);[7] and, most relevant for this discussion, what others know about you but you don't know about yourself (blind area). It is by diminishing our blind area through feedback that we can grow most effectively as employees, as managers, and as human beings.

ACTIVITY 10

The key mechanism for reducing the blind area of your own Johari Window is feedback – feedback from other people. If we often cannot see our own faults, vices, habits, and peculiarities, then sure as eggs is eggs, others see them very clearly! So, if we are to be proactive in acquiring feedback we need to ask for it. Sources at work and elsewhere where feedback is appropriate include: induction, mentoring, counselling, appraisal, line and performance management, meetings, training, interviews, various technologies and social media, and social situations. Choose one or two of these areas and *ask* for feedback about yourself or your performance, or just for helpful pointers to improve what you do.

Given the importance, then, of these three life elements of Relationship, Achievement, and Growth (RAG) – and also the fact that they are core to motivational profiling and the motivators themselves, which effectively have properties aligned with them – what else can we say about them? Quite a lot, actually!

First, there is a clear correlation between the three elements of motivation and the three core modes of human perception. The three basic or core modes of human perception are commonly called Feel, Think, and Know, and there are various websites dedicated to this knowledge.[8] This tripartite structure (three again) derives, according to Hyland, from the very structure of our brains.[9] So Feeling resides in the limbic region of the brain, Thinking in the outer cortex where the 'grey matter' is, and Knowing lies in the basal region just above the spinal column. No one modality is better than another, although we tend to have a preference for one or two of them; as with the Motivational Maps, context determines which is the most appropriate to deploy. So for all of us who are not perfect they are not aligned and not in balance; we tend to have a dominant mode of perception and a backup, secondary one. However, the third modality tends to be weak and ignored, and is our Achilles heel as we become too reliant on our dominant mode and its support.

Feel, Think, Know is about how we like to process information, which in turn affects how we communicate. In essence, and in a simplified form, some people prefer to process information through Thinking, or via the Head. They have, therefore, a predilection for data, words, numbers, facts, detail, analysis, statistics, evidence, proof, and references as their way of communicating and understanding; they are analytical and tend to be intellectual. I like to call this a head-orientation or preference. The danger here is paralysis by over-analysis and ignoring the people factor.

Others prefer to process information through Feeling, or via the Heart. They have, therefore, a predilection for energy, emotions, stories, pictures, anecdotes, examples, graphs, diagrams, and metaphors as their way of communicating and understanding; they are emotional and tend to be creative. I like to call this a heart-orientation or preference. The danger here is loss of focus and lack of hard information for decision-making.

Finally, others prefer to process information through Knowing, or via the Body or Gut, or what the Chinese call the *Dan Tien* – the centre point of the body. They have, therefore, a predilection for the instinctive, the intuitive, the 'gut instinct', decisiveness, relevance, simplicity, immediacy, vision, and certainty as their way of communicating and understanding; they are active and tend to be focused. I like to call this a gut-orientation. The danger here is jumping to conclusions and not appreciating ambiguity.

As we said before, but need to stress, people tend to have a dominant mode and a backup secondary way of processing information; thus, their weak link tends to be their third mode.

ACTIVITY 11

Feel, Think, and Know: what do you think or see or feel as being your correct rank order? Do you prefer processing information intellectually and analytically, or emotionally and creatively, or instinctively and decisively? Keep in mind that all rank orders, like Motivational Map rank orders, are good; but there are consequences, which we call Strengths and Weaknesses, in all preferences.

1. *Preferred* = Think or Feel or Know?

2. *Secondary* = Think or Feel or Know?

3. *Least favourite* = Think or Feel or Know?

What are the consequences of realising these preferences? What are the consequences of your under-utilising one of these modalities? What situations have arisen where your least favourite modality might have been more effective? What action/steps might you take to mitigate this 'Achilles heel'?

Ideally, for Feel, Think, and Know people would have a dynamic balance between their three modes of perception; but this rarely happens, if at all. With Motivational Maps we get the phenomenon we call 'hygiene factors' with the lowest, or sometimes even lower, motivators. This term is explained in Chapter 4 (and see Figure 4.9), but in essence what it refers to is that not having a specific motivator in one's top three profile, and which is especially low scoring, can result in underperformance. So too with the least favourite mode of perception: information that comes via this mode – the least favourite – will tend to be overlooked or ignored, which can become problematic.

But before we go any further we might ask ourselves what other model, aside from Motivational Maps, does the Feel, Think, and Know model remind us of? And the answer of course is the Enneagram: nine numbers in three groups of three that correlate with the head, the heart, and the gut or body. So three motivators are dominantly aligned with our Feel state, our heart, and these can only be our Relationship motivators, for obvious reasons. Three motivators are dominantly aligned with our Think state, our head, and these can only be our Achievement motivators. And finally, three motivators dominantly aligned with our Know state, our gut or body, and these can only be our Growth motivators.

Enneagram	Motivational Map Element	Feel-Think-Know
Heart: Personalities 2 & 3 & 4	Relationships: De & Fr & St	Feel
Head: Personalities 5 & 6 & 7	Achievement: Di & Bu & Ex	Think
Gut: Personalities 8 & 9 & 1	Growth: Cr & Sp & Se	Know

Figure 3.7   Maps, Enneagram, Feel, Think, Know chart

We are, therefore, predicting – and have found in practice – that the Maps do indeed correlate with Feel, Think, and Know. People who have Relationship-dominant motivators will tend to be Feel orientated, and so on. But we need to qualify this because Feel, Think, and Know isn't itself 'one' thing: people tend to have two of the three modes, with one dominant, and these may be similarly or distantly intense whilst the third is relatively inactive. Take that into account alongside the fact that many people have all three motivational types in their top three motivational profile, then identifying clearly their Feel, Think, and Know from the Motivational Map is not going to be an exact science. But, that said, there is a general 'sympathy', if you will, between the two models and they resonate together, if not always perfectly.

With this in mind, let's reconsider the three modes by clearly locating them within the body; also, it's useful to regard them chronologically. Thus, before we could think or know at all (as 'embryos'), all we could do was Feel. We did not 'think' as embryos, or 'know' while in the embryonic state. Our primary mode of perception, then, was and is feeling. If we consider the three life elements, Feeling is most appropriate and useful in the Relationship element. This also explains why Relationship motivators occupy the base of the Maslow Hierarchy. Feeling has primacy and Feeling and relationships go hand in hand. When we no longer 'feel' something for someone, it is almost blindingly obvious that the relationship is at an end. The heart is traditionally where feelings are located (as well, interestingly, as the soul) and because it lives in our pre-conscious reality it can truly be said that feelings are rooted in our past, or more exactly in our precognitive past.

Once we grow beyond infancy, the next mode of perception kicks in: we think about 'stuff'. We have a feeling, but we think as awareness of the feeling grows that 'I'm hungry'. As we grow our need to think becomes more and more important. Often what we feel is discarded or discounted because what is thought is much more important. Schools are places that by and large, with few honourable exceptions, teach us to think and slowly, piece by piece, erode our sense of our feelings' significance. Examinations take most of the feeling away – except the horror before – and reward us for demonstrating 'thinking' skills. Work goes on to do the same; and we start thinking about what we are going to achieve most usually at work, and so the second life element starts to predominate in ways that perhaps distort 'reality'. (The perception of reality will always have consequences of course.) Clearly, thinking is located in the head – the brain. It plans ahead, but it lives primarily in the moment now, the present, where it works out the puzzles that present themselves.

Finally, our third mode of perception is Knowing; this is not thinking. As we are going to see about these modes, they have different tempos or speeds. It takes a while to register and understand what we are feeling. Thinking is quicker, but takes as long to do as the thinking – the ratiocination, the logic – takes, whereas knowing is immediate. In colloquial parlance we talk of 'gut instinct', and that it is where knowing is located: in the gut, or, more precisely as the Chinese would say, the *Dan Tien*, the energy centre of the whole body. The Japanese call this the *Hara*. And this is clearly connected with our self or growth life element. This is instant and it would seem to be either some direct access to knowledge that is almost inexplicable in rational terms, or is some fusion of our thoughts and feelings processed in a way that by-passes their more cumbersome mechanisms. It is partly for this reason and partly because of its outcomes that knowing might be said to be a perceptual mode with a future orientation: knowing – intuition, for example – tells us to do or not to do something, often on the basis of what will happen but has not yet been revealed. This is quite an extraordinary human perception because those who believe in and act on their 'knowing' – their gut, their instinct, their intuition – invariably swear by the accuracy of its results.

Thus in describing Feel, Think, and Know I am also describing potential properties of the Motivational Maps: a Map profile tells us not only about the motivators of the individual (and team and organisation as we shall see), but also points towards their modes of perception orientation.

Further, just as the Maps are aligned with Feel, Think, and Know, so also these are correlated with Speed, Risk, and Change. This is a pretty big claim, so how can this be? First, because when you think about it, energy is about a transfer, an activation of something to somewhere else. And energy has different speeds even in the physical world. Thus, the speed of light is faster than the speed of sound.

With this in mind, we come now to the point of connecting these dots that we have painted. Of the three life elements we find, first, our Relationships. We want to know how to get 'strokes' in our relationships.[10] Relationships are 'slow' in speed terms, take time to form, and are intimately connected to our primary sense of feeling. It should be clear that since they are the foundation of our life, people who are relationship driven tend to be slow to make decisions that might jeopardise their key relationships; also, they will be risk-averse and change-resistant. Why? Because it is critical – certainly at a 'feeling' level – that our relationships do not change, and are not put at risk. Put another way: we do not like the idea that those who love us might withdraw their love or that it will be compromised in some way. Thus, Relationship-type motivator people are 'people' orientated and relationships, which depend primarily on trust, take time and we are naturally averse to quickly undoing them.

Achievement – or Work – elements are medium in speed terms. We think about what we need to do, and then often plan to get it done. Things that we think about do not touch us to the quick in the way that things we feel about do. Also, if we want to achieve anything we recognise, and surely think, something must change here. So, Achievement-orientated individuals will tend to be fairly change-friendly, and moderately risk-positive. They will consider the risks involved in change and take them on board if the plan seems well founded. Thus, Achievement-type people are 'thing' orientated and prefer objectivity, which depends on analysis and so can be accomplished in a reasonable time frame.

Growth (or Self) motivators are much more immediate in speed terms – in fact, fast. Because they are fast, and because less thought and planning go into the mix, they tend to be very risk-friendly and pro-change. They act on instinct, which is risky but which also can be decisive. Because they like change so much, steady states bore them – they need stimulation. So they will tend to be initiators of change at all times. And Growth-type people are 'idea' orientated.

Motivational Map Element	Change/Risk	Speed	Focus
Relationships: (De & Fr & St)	Averse/Avoidance	Slow	People
Achievement: (Di & Bu & Ex)	Mildly Pro/Calculated	Medium	Things
Growth: (Cr & Sp & Se)	Friendly/Positive	Fast	Ideas

Figure 3.8   **Comparing motivators with speed/risk/change, people/things/ ideas**

If we look back over our third chapter, we see that all these ideas link with the Maslow Hierarchy and the motivators. Knowing the motivators gives us a handle on the three life elements, the three modes of perception – the speed, risk, and change tendencies of individuals – and of teams and even whole organisations.

Summary

1.   There are well over 1 million possible motivational profiles.

2.   The nine motivators each have their own distinctive needs, wants, and desires.

3.   The nine motivators correlate with Maslow's Hierarchy of Needs.

4.   There are no good or bad motivational profiles, only contextual ones.

5.   The three core elements of our life – Relationships, Achievement, and Growth – need to be in balance.

6.   Self-awareness enables Growth.

7.   The three modes of human perception – Feeling, Thinking, and Knowing – are aligned with the nine motivators.

8.   Invariably, there is a 'hygiene factor' or Achilles heel in our Feeling, Thinking, or Knowing preferences, as there is in our Motivational Map profiles: we need to be aware of our 'weakness' or blind spot.

9.   Speed of decision-making, attitude to risk, and desire for change are also aligned with the nine motivators – as are our orientation to people, things, and ideas.

Notes

1   See Chapter 2 endnote 10.

2   There are many potential problems for all motivators have strengths, but also corresponding weaknesses. But for this particular combination acute problems might be: short-sightedness or failure to consider the longer-term view; burn-out, as the pace will tend to be relentless; lack of creativity and innovation as things can be too procedural and too systematic to allow for the free play and playfulness of intelligence.

3   James Allen, *As a Man Thinketh*, London, 1903: 'Man's mind may be likened to a garden, which may be intelligently cultivated or allowed to run wild; but whether cultivated or neglected, it must and will bring forth. If no useful seeds are put into it, then an abundance of useless weed-seeds will fall therein, and will continue to produce their kind.'

4   'Strokes' here is a technical word, as used in Transactional Analysis, which refers to the initial repetitive physical contact on which the infant depends to live (and without which they will die), but subsequently refers not only to physical but also to emotional contact. We need approval, recognition, and appreciation, to mention three emotional strokes, from others if we are to thrive as human beings. Indeed, William James put it thus: 'The deepest principle of human nature is the craving to be appreciated' – in other words, to be stroked.

5   Viktor E. Frankl, *Man's Search for Meaning*, London: Hodder and Stoughton, 1946.

6   To be fair this quotation also has another interpretation: namely, knowing oneself means knowing that one is human and not a god, so that one should know one's limitations and not exercise hubris.

[7] Because this area is unknown does not mean, of course, that we forget about it – it is where epiphanies and shared discoveries can occur.

[8] For example http://www.thinkfeelknow.com; also see http://www.shirlawscompass.com/tfk and https://www.trainingjournal.com/articles/feature/think-feel-know.

[9] Clive Hyland, Feature, 1 July 2013; https://www.trainingjournal.com/articles/feature/think-feel-know. Many experts on this topic refer to it as Think-Feel-Know in that order, which makes sense from the structure of the brain perspective. However, I prefer to call it Feel-Think-Know in order to reflect the order of alignment with the Motivational Maps and Maslow.

[10] For more on strokes and Feel-Think-Know see Chapter 7.

Chapter 4

Mapping Your Motivation

We know there are nine motivators and that three of them are dominant in any one individual's profile, so the question becomes: how do we work out what the profile is? There are various ways to do this, and this chapter covers three of them. What we are doing is showing you how to do this for yourself, or for a coach or manager to do this for an employee, as well as doing it electronically. It must be stressed at the outset that the only way to know for sure what your motivational profile is with 100% accuracy is to do the online diagnostic, and more details of this are to be found in Activity 5 in this chapter. But the Motivational Card Game and the Motivational Maps' Quick Technique are also useful and can be 70–80% accurate if done carefully and thoughtfully.

Thus, the first way is the Motivational Card Game, and this is simple. It was developed by the Motivational Maps' Practitioner, Howard Rose. Simply create a card, like a playing card, for each of the nine motivators. The text for each motivator can be found in Figure R.1 in the Resources section of this book; that figure can be photocopied or used to produce examples that can be cut up and laminated. Figure 4.1 shows one example of the card for the nine motivators.

ACTIVITY 1

You will need to create your own playing cards or counters. The wording on each card – e.g. 'Seeks security, predictability, stability' (this is the wording of the Defender card, but the same language pattern is used for all nine motivators) – is from Figure 1.1/3.1. Thus having created your nine cards you are ready to begin.

Sort the nine motivator cards in order of their importance to you. Make a written record of your rank ordering of the cards.

1. What are your top three motivators?
2. How does the overall profile match, or not, your current work role?
3. How consistent or at odds are your top and bottom motivators?
4. How satisfied are you that the needs of your top motivators are currently being met?
5. What would you like to change about your role?

Figure 4.1   Defender card for motivation game

The above questions, if answered honestly, will give you some considerable insight into your current situation at work and the role that you do and how satisfying you find it. A few notes, then, on the five points. First, the top three motivators are crucial for your well-being at work; if they are being fully met, then you are going to be extremely satisfied with your job or your role. Second, when we ask about 'matching' your role, what we mean is think how it provides (or not) opportunities to satisfy the motivator. To give three simple examples: if you were a Defender you would want job security, but what if your job was constantly under threat of being axed? Or, if you were a Builder you would want an above average rate of pay, but suppose you are being paid under the norm for your type of job? And finally, suppose you had Spirit motivator in your profile, but you were in a position where you were swamped with bureaucratic paperwork and had no discretionary time. Ask yourself, does my profile match my role or what I really have to do all day?

Third, when we talk of consistency at the top and bottom what we are referring to is the organic connectedness of the motivators. We already know that they have properties beyond just motivation: Feel, Think, Know; Slow v.

Fast; Risk and Change, to mention three. Suppose, then, you have Creator and Defender as motivator nos 1 and 2 in your profile. In other words, you want change because you like to innovate *and* you like not to change because you want stability: then you have an internal conflict because two fundamental desires are pulling in opposite directions. This can lead, of course, to indecision. But on the other hand, if Creator were no. 1 and Defender were no. 9, then the lowest would reinforce the tendency of the highest motivator because it is distant from it. We will say more about this later in Chapter 6 where it is acutely important when we consider how teams function.

Question 4 simply requires that you be candid with yourself. From the analysis that you have already done, what is emerging? If you are not happy then you need to be clear about it, and this should help you pinpoint exactly what is wrong. Finally, question 5 invites you to speculate on how your role could be better. If you work for yourself, then you can immediately get to work on changing things; if you are an employee, you can begin to frame what you want to discuss with your manager. And to help you get even more specific about this, see Activity 2 and complete the grid.

ACTIVITY 2

Complete the following grid:

	Top Motivators	Current Satisfaction at Work /10	How Improve?
1			
2			
3			

Figure 4.2   Improving your top three motivators

What will you do as a result of it?

A second tool for establishing your motivational profile is one that again you can do on your own, but it is even more accurate if you work in pairs with someone. The Motivational Quick Technique is ideal for coaches and managers who are working one-to-one with people, and who wish to get some sort of 'fix' on what is motivating them. By virtue of somebody else asking you the relevant questions there is a sense of greater objectivity in the answers.

ACTIVITY 3

The process is iterative. Each motivator must be compared with the other eight in turn. In Figure 4.3 tick the blank second column if you choose the motivator, Security (in the first column), or tick the blank fourth column if you choose the motivator in the third column. Go down the column and choose between Security and the other eight motivators. Then do exactly the same with Figures 4.4, 4.5, and 4.6.

CHOOSE			CHOOSE	
Security	Belonging		Belonging	Recognition
Security	Recognition		Belonging	Control
Security	Control		Belonging	Money
Security	Money		Belonging	Expertise
Security	Expertise		Belonging	Innovation
Security	Innovation		Belonging	Autonomy
Security	Autonomy		Belonging	Making a Difference
Security	Making a Difference		7 choices for Belonging v other motivators	
8 choices for Security v other motivators				

Figure 4.3   Motivational Quick Technique – Security/Belonging

To help you compare the motivators with each other, go through each of the Figures 4.4–4.6 using the following sentence stems:

'At work I prefer: Security or Belonging?'

'At work I prefer: Security or Recognition?'

'At work I prefer: Security or Control?'

In this way all the possible choices of motivational preference are exhausted.

It is important not to allow either yourself, if you are doing it on yourself, or your partner (that could be a colleague at work), if you are asking them, to agonise too long over the choices. Usually, your intuitive sense of the correct choice is right.

ACTIVITY 3 (cont.)

CHOOSE		CHOOSE	
Recognition	Control	Control	Money
Recognition	Money	Control	Expertise
Recognition	Expertise	Control	Innovation
Recognition	Innovation	Control	Autonomy
Recognition	Autonomy	Control	Making a Difference
Recognition	Making a Difference		
6 choices for Recognition v other motivators		5 choices for Control v other motivators	

Figure 4.4   Motivational Quick Technique – Recognition/Control

CHOOSE		CHOOSE	
Money	Expertise	Expertise	Innovation
Money	Innovation	Expertise	Autonomy
Money	Autonomy	Expertise	Making a Difference
Money	Making a Difference		
4 choices for Money v other motivators		3 choices for Expertise v other motivators	

Figure 4.5   Motivational Quick Technique – Money/Expertise

CHOOSE		CHOOSE	
Innovation	Autonomy	Autonomy	Making a Difference
Innovation	Making a Difference		
2 choices for Innovation v other motivators		1 choices Autonomy v other motivators	

Figure 4.6   Motivational Quick Technique – Innovation/Autonomy

Each time it is important to say the full sentence when providing the contrasting pairs: 'At work I prefer X or Y.' In total there are 36 choices to make. It is important to stress that this is only a rough and ready guide; it may only be about 70% accurate, and certainly nowhere near as accurate as the full Motivational Map diagnostic (which is described next), but it will give some idea and usually gets two out of the three top motivators correctly identified.

ACTIVITY 4

Now calculate what your top three motivators are. Use the table in Figure 4.7 to do so. You will need to add up the total number of ticks you have allocated to each motivator across the full spectrum of motivators as in Figures 4.4–4.6 in order to do this.

MOTIVATOR	NAME	SUM - *TOTAL No TIMES EACH MOTIVATION IS SELECTED IN THE 36 PAIR CHOICES*	RANK 1^{St}, 2nd, 3rd *USE = FOR EQUAL*
Security	Defender		
Belonging	Friend		
Recognition	Star		
Control	Director		
Money	Builder		
Expertise	Expert		
Innovation	Creator		
Autonomy	Spirit		
Making a Difference	Searcher		

Figure 4.7   Calculate your top three motivators

Where you have two scores which are equal, then the tiebreaker is by re-examining what happened when you contrasted them. The one you choose will have precedence on this occasion. If there are three or more equal scores (within your top three), then that too is interesting; it suggests in the first instance that you are balanced in your motivators. Put another way, many things motivate you. Make an intuitive decision reviewing the choices as to what their rank order is for you. To really know you will have to do a full Motivational Map.

Finally, we come to the single most important and accurate way to establish your motivational profile: completing a Motivational Map online. This takes about 10–15 minutes to do and generates a 15-page report outlining your motivators and how motivated you are. It also gives you important ideas – reward strategies – on how to motivate yourself further or to sustain motivation.

To access your Motivational Map you will need to email Motivational Maps Ltd (info@motivationalmaps.com) and supply the following information:

your name: e.g. Mary Smith

your email address: e.g. mary@tellmeyouremailaddress.com

where you purchased the book: e.g. Amazon.com, Waterstones.

You will then need to supply us with the code word that tells us that you have read the book. Read on for more information.

Within 48 hours of receipt of this information you will receive instructions and a password that will enable you to do a Motivational Map and to receive the report instantly on completion.

ACTIVITY 5

The code word to activate our sending you a password/link is the seventh word of the sentence in the first endnote (endnote 1) of this chapter.[1] Once you have the password/link, complete your Motivational Map.

Now you have your Map here are some pointers for you to look out for. First, your personal motivational audit (PMA) score on page 13 of your Map. This tells you how motivated you are as a percentage score. Naturally, being a percentage score this is very specific, but the important thing is not so much the exact score but which quadrant it is in.

There are four quadrants of motivational 'energy' (just as there are four quadrants of performance), and this is for a very good reason. Basically, the Pareto Principle speaks of an 80:20 relationship underpinning results; this is a 4 to 1 ratio.[2] What this means, therefore, is that we can categorise your motivation into one of four levels or quadrants.

If you have scored over 80% (the result to be found on page 13 of your Map) in your Map, then you are in Quadrant 1, or the Optimal Zone of motivation. This, if sustained, will lead to high performance. Keep in mind that, according to Lou Adler,[3] arguably the world's number one expert on recruitment, high energy is the universal success factor; but, as we established earlier, high motivation and high energy are virtual synonyms.

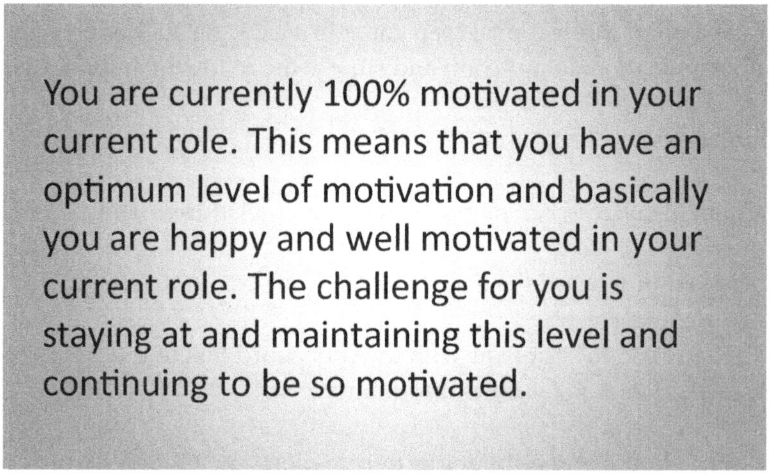

You are currently 100% motivated in your current role. This means that you have an optimum level of motivation and basically you are happy and well motivated in your current role. The challenge for you is staying at and maintaining this level and continuing to be so motivated.

Figure 4.8 Motivational score text

If you have scored between 60% and 80%, then you are in Quadrant 2, the Boost Zone, and this means that you have high energy but are not yet in the Optimal Zone – one or two factors are causing your energy not to be charged, or to be drained away. Usually, if you are in Quadrant 2 this means some minor tweaking in order to boost yourself and get back in the zone.

0%
35%
60%
80%
100%
Action Zone
Risk Zone
Boost Zone
Optimal Zone

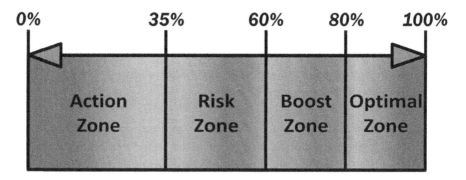

Figure 4.9 The four quadrants of motivation

If you have scored 35–60%, then you are in Quadrant 3, or the Risk Zone of motivation. Some serious demotivation is occurring, and to correct this may involve more than simple tweaking. Often more structural or systemic changes are necessary to reverse the downward flow of your energy.

Finally, if you have scored less than 35% then you are in Quadrant 4, or the Action Zone of motivation. This is a serious situation to be in, as effectively you will be completely unhappy or dissatisfied with your role or job at root level. Comprehensive changes are necessary to revitalise you; or, if that is not possible, then quitting is probably necessary in the longer run.

It must be said that we are not advocating people leave their jobs because of a low motivational score of below 35%, or that management attempts to remove employees who fall below this threshold score as if it were a performance or productivity indicator. On the contrary. First things first: a low motivational score like this requires careful examination with the view to correcting the conditions which caused it and failed to supply sufficient motivation. There is much that can be done. But it must be said too that employees who continue to work over long periods of time when they have absolutely no or little motivation not only damage their organisation through poor performance, but also themselves through stress.

Before we move on to what to do about your motivational profile we need to cover one other intriguing topic: the topic of your lowest motivator, or, more exactly, your lowest motivators, since there may be more than one which play a decisive role in your performance in your role or at work. What we are talking about here is what, according to your profile, does not motivate you, or may even be a motivational aversion. Why is this important?

ACTIVITY 6

Before reading my explanation as to why your lowest motivator is crucial, list all the reasons that you can think of that throw light on why your lowest motivator is important.

Your lowest motivational score can be very revealing. The top three scores are more exciting, but noting our lowest motivator can also give useful clues about improving our motivation and our life.

First, ask the question: is my lowest motivator causing me a problem? We sometimes call this a 'hygiene factor',[4] which means that the motivator does not motivate us, but its absence can lead to demotivation. For example, imagine you are a manager, and Director is your lowest motivator; might that be a problem – needing, but not wanting, to manage? To give another example, suppose your lowest motivator is Builder and your role is a sales role with a low initial salary made up with commissions; in short, money does not motivate you but you are only being offered money to motivate you. For sophisticated readers of the Motivational Map there can be more than one hygiene factor.

Secondly, the lowest motivator may also reinforce all or one of your top three motivators. We call this 'polarity reinforcement'. For example, the Creator is very change-friendly; on the other hand, the Defender is change-averse. If your top motivator is Creator and your bottom is Defender you will be even more change-friendly than if you simply had Creator as number one. It's like a double-whammy effect. The same, of course, would be true in reverse: if Defender were top (change-aversion high) and Creator (change-friendly) were lowest, then the effect would be to strengthen one's resistance to change. There are many examples of possible polarity reinforcements, especially between the Relationship and Growth motivators, which tend to move in opposite change directions anyway; but it also occurs between, say, the Director, who wants control – which thereby restricts autonomy – and the Spirit, who wants to be free. So a Director top motivator with Spirit lowest will give a profile of someone who does not need discretionary time, or even their own space.

Thirdly, your lowest motivator can affect how you feel about others, and so your role within a team. For example, if your lowest motivator is Star and you are working with someone whose top motivator is Star, then it is highly likely, especially in the absence of one or two shared motivators, that you will find their 'attention-seeking' behaviour, as you see and define it, extremely irritating. Indeed, when the score for the lowest motivator is particularly low, below 10 and even below 5, then the motivator is often an aversion. Many conflicts between people in teams are often erroneously identified as 'personality' conflicts when in fact they are motivational conflicts: two or more people have energies that are going in diametrically opposite directions. This can happen with any motivator. Take even the Searcher motivator, the desire for meaning and purpose and to make a difference; if that is someone's strongly lowest motivator then the customer-service ethic of someone for whom it is vital and the number one motivator might well seem excessive, odious, or servile even, and so on. Remember, these motivators are almost subconscious energies, and they make us feel in ways that are not always rational or logical. Fortunately, the shared language of Motivational Maps can provide an escape route from this submerged conflict, as can the development of your self-awareness as you scan your Map.

Accepting your profile, then, what can you do about your motivation and so ultimately about your performance? Clearly, all wisdom begins, as the ancient Greeks knew, with self-awareness,[5] so that already on this journey you should know more about yourself than when you started. If you have done the Motivational Map you now know to a high degree of accuracy what forces

ACTIVITY 7

If you have done the Motivational Map (or even the Motivational Card Game or Motivational Quick Technique) you will know your lowest motivator. What is it? Think about it: this is what you do not want. Given your job or role (or consider a past one), ask yourself whether the absence of this 'want/energy/desire' is likely to be, or has been, problematic for you. Examples might be:

Searcher Lowest	you are in a customer service type of role	Issues?
Spirit Lowest	you are in a role requiring extensive pro-activity and independence	Issues?
Creator Lowest	you are in a role requiring advanced problem solving	Issues?
Expert Lowest	you are in a role needing constant learning upgrades	Issues?
Builder Lowest	you are in a role that is highly competitive and financially driven	Issues?
Director Lowest	you are in a role requiring extensive responsibilities	Issues?
Star Lowest	you are in a foreground role requiring extensive personal exposure	Issues?
Friend Lowest	you are in a role where team work is vital	Issues?
Defender Lowest	you are in a role where security and benefits are the biggest factor of the job	Issues?

Figure 4.10   Lowest motivator issues

Use your lowest motivator to reflect on your issues; and when you have done that, review all nine motivators and the issues that might arise for anyone.

actually motivate or drive you. That's good. You need to bear in mind that motivators change over time. I usually advocate doing a Motivational Map once every two years to track changes; but, given all this, what then?

Now begins the hardest part – where we commit to change.[6] We embrace the idea that we have motivators – needs, wants, desires – and that we have given them names. 'Feeding' these motivators is what is going to turn us 'on'; or, to use another metaphor, our motivators are effectively hot buttons into our psyche: they switch us 'on'. To make this really clear, let's consider the most obvious of the motivators: the Builder. It is the most obvious because it is arguably the most tangible. What does the Builder want? Money! (And a little more besides: to win, for example.) So what will increase the Builder's motivation, the Builder's energy, and the Builder's drive? Money! It's that simple, but also that difficult.

Consider there are nine motivators and nearly everyone has three motivators which are dominant at any one time in their profile.[7] Thus, as a starting point, no one 'thing' will necessarily motivate or provide the spur that somebody needs to increase their energy. At the same time, we can be reasonably confident that by feeding any one of the three dominant motivators this will have an effect. So the question becomes: what is the core activity that underpins or underlies each motivator? What generic description of the activity meets the need, the want, the desire – the motivator?

ACTIVITY 8

Look at Figure 4.11 and see if you can establish what activity would most meet or satisfy the motivator. I have done the first one for you. The Searcher seeks meaning and purpose, and is specifically motivated by wanting to make a difference. So the key 'thing' that would motivate such a person with that motivator is 'knowing that they have made that difference'; and the most generic description of that condition is receiving quality feedback. In other words, the Searcher motivator loves receiving quality feedback, and this motivates them to even higher levels of motivation and so performance. To be clear, then: we all – all nine motivators – might like quality feedback, but that doesn't mean it motivates us in the way it motivates the Searcher. Put another way, quality feedback is 'nice' for all of us, but it is essential for the Searcher if we want the Searcher to be highly motivated.

Motivator	Hot Button	Key Motivation Action
Searcher	Meaning & Making a Difference	Access Quality Feedback
Spirit	Freedom & Independence	?
Creator	Innovation & Change	?
Expert	Expertise & Mastery	?
Builder	Money & Material Satisfaction	?
Director	Power & Influence	?
Star	Recognition & Respect	?
Friend	Belonging & Friendship	?
Defender	Security & Predictability	?

Figure 4.11   Key motivation actions[8]

I call the activities that boost motivation 'Reward Strategies', and everyone needs to actively consider reward strategies for their life on a regular and ongoing basis. Basically, we – most of us – can see the need for physical exercise as a mechanism for sustaining our fitness or physical health;[9] so here we are talking about sustaining our emotional health, or our internal energy, by doing the right kind of things, or enabling the right sort of situations, to be part of our daily environment. In this way we can stay emotionally healthy.

A Personal Development Plan, or PDP,[10] is a well-known feature of development programmes for individuals within and without organisations; but they mostly focus on skill and knowledge acquisition. It's a good idea, then, to consider a PDP for yourself that focuses on your motivation. Remember that the complete loss of all motivation is not a typical experience save in the medical extremity of depression. Loss of motivation tends not to happen in one tsunami, but happens gradually; there is a slow chipping away usually, and one can almost be unaware of it.

To realise the truth of this remark one only has to consider what happens when most people start a new job.[11] On Day 1 their motivation is often 100%, and it stays that way for several months. Indeed, it can resemble a share price that starts strong, but slowly and inevitably its price drifts downwards; and before one is scarcely aware of it, as there has been no big headline or crisis, the company is worth a lot less. Indeed, the share price dips and dips, and then the company is in danger of full collapse, just as the individual's motivation is in danger of full collapse as he or she enter the Action Zone of motivation. And whose fault is it? It may be the individual's, but more often the organisation itself has failed to motivate the employee, or even considered motivating them part of their responsibilities – just as ultimately management is responsible for the slide of the share price.

With this is mind you may wish to revisit Figure 4.2 to see whether there is more you can do to boost your motivators.

ACTIVITY 9

Revisit Figure 4.2 (Improving your top three motivators) and now ask yourself these questions:

How does your current role fulfil your three motivators? If it doesn't, then why not and how doesn't it?

How can you get more motivated?

How can your manager or boss enhance your current role?

How can you support and help motivate other team members?

Finally, then, given the generic motivational actions we have outlined, what about more specific and small-scale actions? Here are some ideas for Reward Strategies that involve small things to self-motivate. They are grouped in their RAG cluster.

Motivator	Example Of Reward Strategy
Searcher	Actively seek out positive, quality feedback. You thrive on feedback, so make sure you get some, and don't overlook social media: Facebook can easily be a vehicle for quality feedback, and tools like Linkedin have a 'Recommendation' facility which is ideal.
Spirit	Develop the mind-set that you are really the Managing Director or Chief Executive of your own business. Your current employer is simply your biggest client or customer, and that is temporary anyway.
Creator	Take a 'sabbatical' – one hour, one day, one week, one month, one year – and do something entirely different. Re-charge and replenish your personal batteries.
Expert	Make sure – insist – your appraisal discussions not only include goal setting, but also training opportunities to help you achieve organisational and personal goals.
Builder	Motivate yourself by giving yourself small 'perks' whenever you achieve your own targets: these can be whatever you want or like – a glass of wine, a bar of chocolate, a luxury and relaxing bath, and so on.
Director	Use an external career consultant to help you map out your ideal career over the next few years
Star	Reset your targets. Make them more ambitious and clearly lined to high visibility rewards
Friend	Greet people on a daily basis – you like this, and usually they like it too. When you meet someone, smile and make strong eye contact – this is good advice for dealing with everybody, but as a Friend you will find this particularly effective.
Defender	Allocate one hour a week to tidy your office, your space, and do filing – or if not in an office, consider your equivalent. This can have a big effect on your productivity and anyway creates a greater sense of order, and so of security.

Figure 4.12   Motivator Reward Strategies[12]

With the all the ideas and information you have now received, and if you have completed the various action points (especially the Motivational Map), then you should be in a great position to complete your own MAP or Motivational Action Plan. A simple template for this is found on page 14 of the individual Motivational Map.

ACTIVITY 10

Complete your own MAP.

Motivational Action Plan

My Goals

What will I do?	How will I do it?	When will I do it?

Figure 4.13   Motivational Action Plan

Summary

1. There are three ways you can establish your Motivational Map profile.

2. The least accurate method, but most fun, is the Motivational Card Game.

3. Underpinning your motivational profile is the assumption that you wish to and can improve your motivational satisfaction.

4. The Motivational Quick Technique is the second method, and this is especially useful when done in pairs; in other words, it can be effective when managing or coaching.

5. The truly accurate and best method for establishing your motivational profile is by doing a Motivational Map online, and you can do this by following my instructions in Activity 5 of this chapter whereby you can access this opportunity.

6. There are four quadrants of motivation/performance, and the online Map establishes in which quadrant you fall and what that means for you.

7. Your lowest motivator is also significant because of 'hygiene factors', 'polarity reinforcements', and team integration.

8. Reward Strategies are used to impact and increase motivation.

9. Reward Strategies – one for each motivator – are supplied as ideas to help you self-motivate.

Notes

1 'The soul, being the source of motion, is the most ancient thing there is' – Plato.

2 One of the best books on the Pareto Principle and its applications for organisations and business is Richard Koch, *The 80/20 Principle: The Secret of Achieving More with Less*, London: Nicholas Brealey, 2007.

[3] Lou Adler, *Hire with Your Head: A Rational Way to Make a Gut Reaction*, New York: Wiley, 1998.

[4] I use the term 'hygiene factor' following the work of Herzberg. Herzberg realised that there were aspects of work which, while not motivating in themselves, might, through their absence, be demotivating. For example, nobody is motivated to go to work because of tea and coffee facilities, but if one were to permanently find that the organisation was not interested in providing either refreshments or even a facility where one could make one's own refreshments this might become extremely demotivating over time. Frederick Herzberg, *The Motivation to Work*, New York: Wiley, 1959, and *One More Time: How Do You Motivate Employees?* Boston, MA: Harvard Business Review, 1968. As an interesting sidebar, Herzberg clearly had a great sense of humour, for he came up with the KITA formula too: this he identified as how not to motivate and influence people, KITA being an acronym for the 'Kick in the Ass' approach to management!

[5] See endnote 6 in Chapter 3 for another take on this.

[6] Commitment is an act of will. On the one hand the goal must be valued for it to be pursued with genuine commitment, and on the other hand the likelihood of perceived success in achieving it must be real or high; otherwise, despite its value, there is no point committing because of the perception of likely failure. Clearly, issues of self-esteem are paramount here even in one's ability to commit to anything, since the self-esteem itself is partly made up of our sense of self-efficacy; in other words, our belief that we are able will affect our sense of the likelihood of achievement. Since self-esteem is a component of the self-concept and the self-concept partially drives our motivators, there is a loop here in which the will itself feeds the motivators and is fed by them.

[7] In over 99% of Maps that we see and review there are three dominant motivators, but occasionally a pattern emerges for an individual where clearly there are two or four dominant motivators; and then really rarely there is the person where the numbers indicate only one effective motivator or five. In an introductory work like this, these extremes will not be considered as they require in-depth expertise to spot the numerical patterning that indicates such results.

[8] Here are some ideas in order from the top of Figure 4.11: Spirit – renew your vision; Creator – problem solve through innovation; Expert – seek training and learning; Builder – reset your goals; Director – request more responsibility; Star – work on visibility; Friend – be a friend; Defender – seek clarification.

[9] And let's not forget relationships: the idea that we tell the person we love that 'I love you' once and never do it again is a recipe for disaster. Relationships need to be constantly worked on too – like motivation.

[10] Sometimes called CPD, or Continuing Professional Development; the name is less important than the activity, which is effectively about embracing lifelong learning.

[11] This is probably untrue when one is dealing with employees for whom a job is just that – a job. In these situations there is usually no career structure; the work is often unskilled, monotonous, low status, and very low paid. We can here be returning to that earlier point we made about 'surviving' at the bottom of the Maslow pyramid and where people are too busy surviving to consider or act according to their motivators: see my discussion on Maslow and B- and D-needs in Chapter 3.

[12] Motivational Maps provides over 150 Reward Strategies relevant to the nine motivators for its practitioners to use with their client organisations.

Chapter 5

Motivation and Performance

We come now to the core importance of motivation. Indeed, you may have thought that having spent four chapters outlining how we understand, describe, measure, and reward motivation that we had already reached an important tipping point. If we go back to reflect on Chapter 1 we may remember the particular problem that ambiguity created for most leaders and managers, and how they like to avoid such difficulties. The truth is that organisations, with rare exceptions, tend not to buy motivation. Yes, they say they want it, but it is well down on their Christmas wish list.

In sales-speak motivation is a 'feature',[1] but people and organisations do not buy features; instead, they buy benefits. We talked about these broadly in Chapter 1, but now let's be more specific. So what are the benefits of motivation? It is here that things become really interesting.

> ### ACTIVITY 1
>
> If motivation is a feature of the work experience, what then are the benefits that derive or arise from having motivation in the workforce? Put another way, what do you think organisations and people really want to buy when they say they want 'motivation'? Make a list of the benefits that you can identify both for individuals and for organisations.

On a personal level it is quite clear what the benefits of motivation are. I call them the '3 Es' of motivation. First, there is energy; motivation is synonymous with energy, and everyone feels it is better to have it than not. Second, there is enthusiasm, which is slightly different; but the mere fact of having energy raises one's levels of enthusiasm, and this is an infectiously positive quality. It brings a whole new dimension to work and to the other activities in which we partake; not only do we have energy to cope, but we really want to get stuck in and somehow radiate this fact to others. This strangely makes us more attractive to other people, and so more influential. It might even be contested that enthusiasm is the single most attractive quality in another person, or at least it is the quality that we are most drawn to.[2] Finally, as energy begets enthusiasm, enthusiasm begets engagement: we become not only enthusiastic about what we are doing, but committed too. This is a major benefit to us and our well-being; but it should also be clear that at this point it also becomes a benefit to any organisation for which we happen to work, or a major benefit to our own business if we are self-employed.

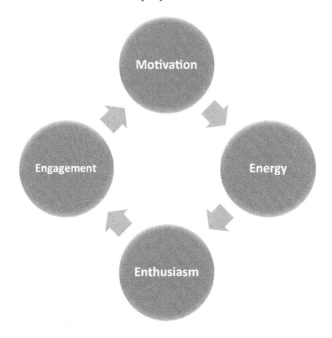

Figure 5.1   Motivation: energy–enthusiasm–engagement

ACTIVITY 2

Give yourself a score out of 10 for the following:

Motivation at work

Energy in work

Enthusiasm for work

Engagement with work

Is there a connection between each of these links in the chain in your experience? If there is, then consider how to boost each of these core benefits. If not, then examine why not? Why, for example, might you score yourself as high in energy but low in enthusiasm? What factors are at work here in your experience?

We arrive, then, at the benefits of motivation for the organisation, and again there are three primary benefits (alongside engagement, which is a definite benefit) which I like to call the '3 Ps'. These follow a natural sequence and I intend to comment on all of them in turn; but the starting point is that motivation is intimately correlated with performance. Organisations want performance from their employees; indeed, as it happens, employees want performance from themselves for the simple reason that our self-esteem is tied to how we perform. Anyone who performs at a poor level for a prolonged period of time in any field feels bad about their self and seeks ways to escape or rationalise their lack of performance. And when I say 'field' I especially mean the field of our relationship: to perform poorly as a husband or wife or partner or sibling or friend, or any such relationship, creates an inordinate strain on us, consciously or otherwise.

What are the ingredients of performance and how is motivation related to it? High performance is characterised by three outstanding elements: first, a clear sense of direction. Direction at an organisational level refers to the organisational vision, mission, goals, objectives, plans, and strategies; on a personal level, direction means one's career aspirations and plans. In both cases, however, failure to set the right course is disastrous, whether or not you have motivation. Motivation per se cannot compensate for the wrong strategy for your life or for your business. Put another way, if you want to win Olympic medals, then you need to swim down the lanes, not across them! There is a sense here of going with the grain of who you are and knowing what your strengths and weaknesses are, and so exploiting and expanding them to the full. Explicating vision and strategy clearly and convincingly is a core part of leadership, and motivation is not a substitute for it; but on their own vision and strategy are not enough.

Performance requires also that we have the relevant knowledge and skills and openness to learning that enable and facilitate high achievement and outstanding outcomes. On a personal development level the American aphorism "To earn more learn more" is profoundly true, as it is organisationally true. Many studies have demonstrated beyond question that organisations that invest in their people outperform those that do not. Indeed, in the UK for the last 20 years or so the Investors in People[3] project has actively traded (and mostly been government funded) on the basis that investing in people's skills and development is the surest way to increased profitability and long-term sustainability. According to them, for example, '60% of Investors in People accredited businesses predict business growth compared to the UK establishment average of 47%'.[4]

Working out what the knowledge and skill gap is for any organisation is a core activity without which poor performance is assured. Employees have to know what they are doing and feel confident in the execution of their skills – whether these are technical, IT, compliance, health and safety, managerial, customer service, sales, or whatever else needs to be done.

ACTIVITY 3

Here is one example of a skills assessment grid, and in this instance it is auditing management and team type skills.

Key Skill	A	B	C	D	Comments Actions
Communicating					
Delegating					
Motivating staff					
Team building					
Inducting staff					
Mentoring					
Planning					
Evaluating training					
Managing change					
Performance review					

Figure 5.2   Management and team skills audit

Notice the four rating categories of A (outstanding), B (excellent), C (good), and D (poor); this anticipates the comments later in this chapter on the Pareto Principle. How do you rate yourself? Which of your skills are strong and where are they weak? Assessing yourself is a powerful tool for personal development; but organisations need to assess you to ensure – in this instance – that your management capability is sufficient for you to be able to perform. Based on your analysis, what actions might you take or initiate?

On their own, however, neither of these two features, direction and skills, is sufficient. The core feature that guarantees that the employee will perform at a high level is motivation – in other words, that particular energy which enables employees to undertake and complete the task or tasks which are necessary to achieve the projects and goals. You can be going in the right direction and have all the skills and knowledge in the world, but if you have no energy then you are not going to get far. This is analogous to a car. You point the steering wheel to advance in the right direction; the engine and chassis are superbly crafted to enable a comfortable ride; but the car has no petrol – no fuel, no gas – and so cannot even get out of the garage.

So performance looks like this:

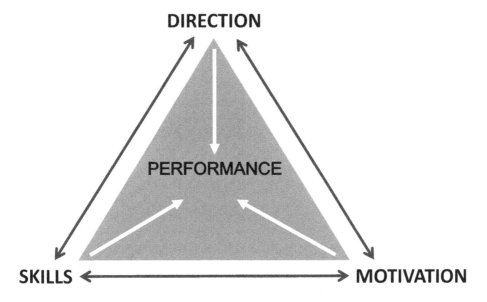

Figure 5.3   Performance pyramid

Given this, something interesting happens, however, when we consider performance at the shop-level. 'Shop-level' here means virtually all levels within an organisation apart from the most senior. What am I getting at? This: that from the organisational point of view most employees have nothing to do with direction or strategy; they have made a personal career choice to join an organisation, and from then on they are being judged not on their contribution to the direction of the organisation, which is very rarely invited, but on how they perform. And so this comes down to the other two elements: skills (and knowledge) and motivation.

We can therefore create a small, rough-and-ready formula, but one which time and again proves to be very accurate, namely: performance = skills ×

motivation. Thus, what if we score ourselves – and others for that matter – on a scale of 1–10, 10 being outstanding or fully motivated or fully skilled/ knowledgeable?

ACTIVITY 4

	Performance %	Skills / 10	Motivation / 10
You			
Peer at Work			
Subordinate			

Figure 5.4   Performance table

Think about your motivation at work over the last three months: out of 10, how would you score yourself? Ten is outstanding/fully charged motivation and 1 would be that you can scarcely be bothered to get out of bed to go to work. Don't agonise – what number pops into your mind? Be honest. Write it down; do the same for your skills and knowledge. Ask yourself how skilful/knowledgeable have you been at work over the last three months in your current role: 10 suggests that you know exactly how to do your job and all aspects of it; 1 suggests that it's as if you were on day one of your employment and everything is confusing. Again, what number springs to mind? Jot it down. You may then want to think about others in your workplace – a peer for example, or somebody you manage. How do they rate? Calculate your performance score as a percentage. What do you learn from this analysis of your performance (and others')?

In broad terms there will be four categories. If you have 80% or over, then you know you are in the 'zone' of performance; if you are in the 60–80% quadrant, then you will be high performing, but there's lots of scope to improve; if you are somewhere between 35% and 60%, then performance is slipping away and you are at best 'good', which really means average; and finally, below 35% and you are in a dangerous quadrant where you know yourself that you are performing poorly and this is draining you – as well as being dangerous for your future career.

And here is something extra that is astonishing when you think about it. The average score we tend to find when we do this in our training sessions with thousands of people is 6. People tend to be motivated 6 out of 10 and skilled 6 out of 10. Six sounds a perfectly reasonable score, doesn't it, but when you multiply the sixes together you get a performance rating of 36% – low indeed. So, average multiplied by average, in other words, equals complete mediocrity.

To be really zinging in performance terms one needs to be a 9 and a 9, to give an 81% performance rating. Thus it is that one must seriously work on motivation in oneself because skill is not enough, as this simple test shows.

If we plot now high and low motivation versus high and low skill set, we end up with four quadrants (see Figure 5.5).

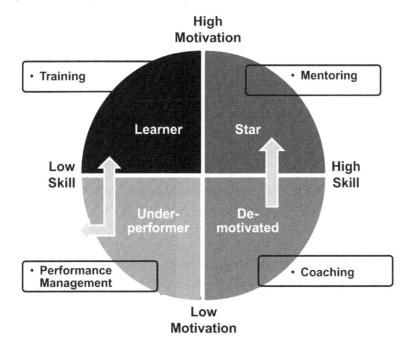

Figure 5.5   Four quadrants of performance

ACTIVITY 5

Review your team(s) and ask yourself in which quadrant you would place each member. Are they 'learners' – low on skill but highly motivated, just as someone new might be who is about to undertake an induction programme? Possibly the single most effective methodology for dealing with learners is training. Or are they 'underperformers', low on skill and motivation, in which case they need to be performance managed? Alternatively, are they 'stars', high on motivation and skill level, in which case we need to keep them and sustain them? Mentoring is possibly the most effective way of maintaining high performance levels. Or finally, are they 'demotivated', the most dangerous quadrant of all? Here we have high skills but low motivation, and typically this can arise with employees who have been around a long time and know the organisation almost too well. They can be very difficult to manage, and probably the most effective way of improving these employees' performance is through a coaching programme.

Keep in mind when you consider these types of employee and where they fit on the quadrants whether training, performance management, mentoring, or coaching is the ideal solution or approach; all of them need to be motivational to have any effect at all. Training that is not motivating is tedious at best and counterproductive at worst; and this is equally true for performance management, mentoring, and coaching. Without that energy which is motivation our best efforts are likely to be futile.

Performance, then, is about being on top of one's work, of being able to achieve things both for oneself and for the organisation; and inevitably, as night follows day, if we perform at a high level for any length of time we start becoming extremely productive. So being productive means that we produce 'stuff': products, services, ideas, innovations, value, and profit. Possibly, then, being productive is the number one thing that employers want from their employees; it is self-evidently mission critical.

What makes a highly productive employee? Who are the highly productive employees? If we remember the Pareto Principle, or the 80/20 Rule, we will be clear that these highly productive individuals can be up to 16 times more productive than their less successful counterparts. Sixteen times![5] That is a staggering achievement, especially if we are dealing with, as we frequently are, people being paid the same standard salary. Further, and awfully, the Pareto Principle also clearly means that 20% of our employees produce 80% of our profit (or value-add) and, sadly, 80% produce only 20%. The challenge, then, is to skew this law so that it works more in our favour: imagine how much more productivity and profit would be possible if, instead of 80–20, we had 70–30 or even 60–40. In other words, imagine what would happen for our organisation if we doubled the number of employees who are seriously productive.

But how do we find these 'productive' individuals? Productivity is a people issue. People make things happen – or not. This seems to be a revelation to some managers, as if merely pushing people around and simply paying them a wage leads to high productivity. The reality is that this approach leads to subtle sabotage and non-vocal resistance: lip-service to the organisations and its goals, but at root a deep dislike and resentment. Eventually, of course, it leads to outright hostility, and then we go down the line of cost: somebody quits and we have to start all over again.[6] Alternatively, bad managers take the view that they can discount their people because technology will do it all – how misguided can one be?

People are in one sense like bees: they like being productive; they like being in a well-tuned hive where everyone and everything has its place and all is purposeful. It produces honey and sweetness, and the sense of a life well spent. But what is productivity and where is it in the scheme of things? Now that's the interesting thing; that's the thing which if all managers understood they might get real about leading their employees instead of just paying them.

Productivity is what it says it is: it is the ability of the individual (and teams) to produce something, to create – be that a product (a thing), a service, or value. In short, productivity is about adding to the sum of existence: something that wasn't there before is now there, and as a direct result of the individual's efforts. You'd think everybody would want to be productive, not least because it boosts one's own self-esteem; but if you think so, you'd be wrong. That said, however, the important thing to grasp is the position of productivity in the scheme of organisational activities.

Productivity sits midway between the two other vital 'Ps': performance and profit. Productivity is the bridge to profits. As Dr Alex Krauer said, 'When people grow, profits grow.' We need high-performing people to start with. We need therefore to focus on recruitment in the first instance, and how we go about it. This topic goes beyond the scope of this book as it requires a whole book to itself to do it justice; but clearly if high energy is the number one success factor in any hire,[7] and energy is motivation, then the Motivational Maps have a tremendous application in this field, since they are measuring at the outset the very thing the recruiters and the organisations claim they are looking for in the candidates.

But clearly, productivity must involve employee performance; there is no way round it. We have to go back to first principles. Yes, we want the profits and we can anticipate and plan for them, but we can't just kick people into being productive; they need to be high-performing individuals and teams. So if we are not happy with our current levels of productivity, then how are we going to change the situation? By doing some serious thinking about the performance of our individuals.

This can be done on an individual level, team level, and at the organisational level. But here is a quick, personal aide-memoir to ask yourself, and then to ask yourself about your employees:

ACTIVITY 6

What one skill, if you had it now, would make the greatest impact on your own productivity? This could be anything – a technical, interpersonal, or strategic skill. Whatever it is, now you've identified it, how are you going to bridge the gap?

Similarly, what one skill if your employees had it now would make the biggest difference to the productivity of the whole? Remember that the whole point about the 'one skill' that would have the greatest impact is that we are invoking the Pareto Principle – a small number of things, one even, can have a disproportionate influence on everything else.

This issue leads on to the more general point about training or learning: nobody stays highly productive for very long. We all need updates and inputs to remain effective. What is true of skills is also true of knowledge. Information is said to have a 'half-life',[8] and this span seems to be decreasing in most disciplines, which means knowledge is increasingly out of date and irrelevant.[9] So, 50% of what we know will be redundant within a shorter and shorter time frame. To improve productivity, therefore, there must be a mechanism in place to audit the knowledge, skills, and attitudes (or competencies) of all employees.

But that is only half the equation on the individual level – skills are not enough on their own. Employees need to be motivated, and for this too we need an audit; we need Motivational Maps, the world-proven methodology for looking at individual and team motivation. Nobody is saying these audits are easy; what is? If you want results, then you need to drill down into the granular detail of what is happening with your employees, especially at a motivational – that is, at an 'I want' – level.

It's natural that senior managers want to go straight to profits, for profits are real, are tangible, and they are the goal. But to get there we have to defer immediate gratification and explore the mushy soup of motivation, of feelings and wants and people; but if we can do that, the rewards are vast because the productivity gains will be enormous.

ACTIVITY 7

Here are nine generic ways of boosting employee productivity. Review them and apply the Pareto Principle: maybe two or three of these nine ideas might work for you and your organisation. Identify the two or three that you think might work and produce an action plan. Remember, any one of these nine simple ideas may help you increase people productivity.

	9 Productivity Ideas for Employees	Appeals to...
1	*Explain clearly what you want from your employees. One of the biggest problems that obstructs productivity is that people do not know what they're really trying to do, what they're trying to achieve, or even why they are doing what they do. So clarity about what it is they're doing is absolutely essential; therefore, in simple terms, communicate, communicate, communicate.*	*This would especially appeal to the Defender motivator type.*
2	*If you want employees to be productive, then you need to motivate the leaders, the team leaders. Without the team leaders themselves being motivated it is highly unlikely employees will be. The best way of all of motivating the team leaders is to run a programme, initially profiling the leaders using Motivational Maps.*	*This would especially appeal to the Star motivator type as it foregrounds them.*
3	*Ask employees for ideas on improving productivity. If they are asked and their ideas are subsequently implemented, this becomes very motivational as they feel ownership. This makes them more productive. So how effectively are you drawing on the expertise and ideas of your own employees? Could you do more?*	*This would especially appeal to the Expert motivator type*

	9 Productivity Ideas for Employees	Appeals to...
4	*Having explained clearly what you want - in other words, communicated effectively - we need to think about simplifying all processes. That we use complicated processes confuses employees, confuses customers. How can we simplify them and how can we make them more user-friendly? Another way of putting it would be making our processes fit for purpose; people like it and are happy when things work the way they are supposed. That happiness translates into bee-hive hums of productivity!*	*This would especially appeal to the Director motivator type.*
5	*Another good way of boosting productivity is to try to define what your customer needs. This has several benefits. First, it stops what might be called mission creep, which is very demoralizing for employees. Employees want to satisfy the customer but with mission creep there is never an end in sight where this might occur! This is demotivating and leads to a drop in productivity. Furthermore, defining the customer need more exactly also leads to greater profitability for the company as the waste of mission creep is avoided. Finally, the more tightly defined the need is, the clearer the objective, and this allows employees a greater chance to deliver it – hence, to be more productive.*	*This would especially appeal to the Friend motivator type.*
6	*Following on from simplifying all processes is to invest in technology, not for the sake of technology, but for the sake of the productivity it can produce. We all know that technology is moving forward at a cracking pace, and we've all seen organizations using old technology on the unstated premise that they are getting a full return on the initial capital investment. But in getting the most from it, and by carrying on using an old technology, which really doesn't serve the customer or the employees well, we find customers move away and employees become less productive.*	*This would especially appeal to the Creator motivator type.*

Figure 5.6   Nine productivity ideas for employees

ACTIVITY 7 (cont.)

9 Productivity Ideas for Employees	Appeals to...
7	Another good idea is to introduce flexi-time into the working environment. One of the issues of primary concern is the idea that it is not the length of time that people work that is really important, or measuring how long they spend at the job, rather how productive they are, or what results they achieve. Clearly we have to draw a line here because some jobs do require time duration rather than simple results: people need to be there for example in manning a shop for certain periods of time. However, that said, it is important to understand that if we can give people some flexibility in their time commitment to the organization, this can be extremely motivating for them because it increases their internal locus of control; this is a major contribution to their sense of freedom and well-being and produces greater levels of productivity.	This would especially appeal to the Spirit motivator type.
8	One central issue is the correlation between pay and performance. Many companies seem to think performance is a secondary reason for why they are paying people; indeed the truth of the matter is that performance is primary. The performance is what drives greater productivity and this, if the strategy is correct, is what leads to enhanced profitability. So the question is: do we have a clear link between pay and performance, one that is fair, equitable, and transparent? Because we need to have.	This would especially appeal to the Builder motivator type.
9	Finally, look at revamping the working environment. This can make such a massive difference to the psychology of people working for you. If your environment is dark, boring, grey, and with other, similar attributes, then you can only expect non-stimulation in your employees, which creates lacklustre performance, and furthermore, and ultimately, a lack of productivity. Investing in a great working environment is investing in them. What do people like? Nature, art, music, colour and general stimulation - the lighting, the quality of air, and so on. What is your environment like? What can you do to improve it? You might want to measure the difference it makes – before and after.	This would especially appeal to the Searcher motivator type.

Figure 5.6   Nine productivity ideas for employees (*concluded*)

Keep in mind two further points about these ideas. First, that although each idea has been allocated a specific motivator that it might especially relate to, many of the ideas touch two or three motivators simultaneously. For example, idea 3, asking for employee suggestions to improve productivity: yes, it appeals to the Expert, but clearly can also strongly appeal to the Creator, and also possibly to the Searcher and Director for different reasons. Second, why not consider the team motivational profile itself as the basis for the selection of the productivity exercises? In other words, if your team has Defender as its number one motivator, then why not consider the first idea, which is the call for clarity?

From this, consider creating an action plan to implement two or three of these ideas which you think could make the greatest difference to productivity. In doing this one further issue remains for you to consider, namely, how will you observe or measure the increase in productivity? You need in other words to benchmark how productive your employees are now, so that the changes can unmistakably demonstrate improvements in productivity.

To think about benchmarking in more depth we can ask ourselves: what does an increase in productivity look like? Figure 5.7 has some great questions to consider in your organisation.

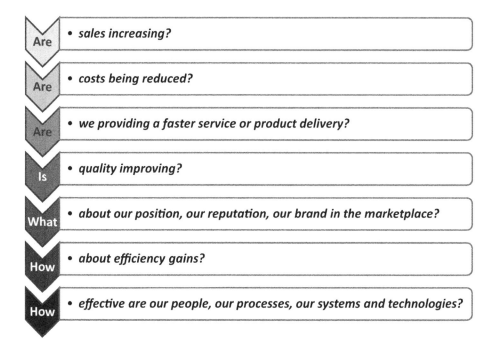

- *sales increasing?*
- *costs being reduced?*
- *we providing a faster service or product delivery?*
- *quality improving?*
- *about our position, our reputation, our brand in the marketplace?*
- *about efficiency gains?*
- *effective are our people, our processes, our systems and technologies?*

Figure 5.7   Productivity questions

Three primary ways of establishing what levels of productivity we have, and so be able to gauge the difference when we implement two or three of the nine ideas, are:

1.   results monitoring (using organisational data)

2.   customer questionnaires or surveys or feedback

3.   employee appraisals.

ACTIVITY 8

Establish what criteria you will use to benchmark the productivity of your employees before implementing a productivity-improvement plan. Decide, too, on what time frames you will use to monitor your progress.

This leads us to the final organisational benefit after performance and productivity, namely, profitability. But you will remember that this benefit came with a caveat: namely, profit follows enhanced performance and increased productivity so long as the strategy was or is right for the organisation. No super performance, no outstanding productivity alone can produce profit if the strategy is wrong for the organisation. History is littered with tens of thousands of organisations – big and small, known and unknown, well-resourced and under-resourced – which have had a superb and productive workforce, but which have failed and gone to the wall.[10]

The failure to adopt the right strategy for an organisation is invariably a failure of leadership and often it comes down to one person, the leader, the CEO or some such, or alternatively the top group; and in this latter case the failure usually has a special aspect to it called 'groupthink'. As George S. Patton put it, 'If everybody is thinking alike, then somebody isn't thinking.'

The problem of groupthink is well recognised.[11] Groupthink is evidence of closed minds, conformity, and conventionality. Sun Tzu expressed the dilemma when he said: 'Take care when everyone disagrees with you. But take even greater care when everyone agrees.' The most famous story as an antidote to groupthink is Peter Drucker's:

> *Alfred P. Sloan [of General Motors] is reported to have said at a meeting of one of his top committees: 'Gentleman, I take it we are all in complete agreement on the decision here.' Everyone around the table nodded in assent. 'Then', continued Mr. Sloan, 'I propose we postpone further discussion of this matter until our next meeting to give ourselves time to develop disagreement and perhaps gain some understanding of what the decision is all about.'*[12]

How to create the right strategy for your organisation is beyond the remit of this book, but there is an aspect of strategy that must be commented on now, and it is this: given the strategy of the organisation, do the dominant motivators of the employees and the employee teams support or detract from the strategy or the direction? Keep in mind what we said before that motivation is energy; more specifically, though, it is nine types of energy and every type has its own direction or 'qualities'. Suppose, then, we have a strategy but the dominant motivators within the organisation are at odds with it. What then? Then we have a problem.

For example, and this is to simplify, for we need to remember that individuals and teams have more than one dominant motivator, suppose our strategy in a service industry is to be niche and to be quality and at a premium price. But then suppose that the motivational profile of our employees (however many that may be, from two to 20,000) has Searcher as the lowest motivator. The Searcher motivator is the most customer-focused of all the nine motivators because the Searcher wants to make a difference for them. Can you see the problem such a profile might generate?

Or again, imagine an IT company whose strategy is around supplying innovative new solutions to its corporate clients. Expert may be the dominant motivator within the organisation (as it often is with 'techies'), but suppose – as happens – Creator is the lowest motivator. What this is saying is that the employees have the ability – the skill set – to innovate, but they don't especially want to. Over time, how might that translate into a problem for the IT organisation in terms of its reputation with its clients?

Finally, one more example: imagine a company whose strategy is built around high sales and volume – stack 'em high and sell 'em cheap – and alongside that commission for sales people. What if the Builder motivator were the lowest motivator for the profile? How would that play out? Again, not to have a large sprinkling of highly competitive, goal-driven, money-orientated people – the Builder – within that kind of strategy betokens all sorts of potential problems ahead.

ACTIVITY 9

Here are three classic business models. Which motivators do you think might drive them most effectively, and which motivators might be problematic if absent (low or lowest scored)?

Collective Business Model

Here a business organisation or association is composed of a relatively large number of businesses or professionals in the same or related fields of enterprise. They share resources, pool information, or can provide other benefits for their members. A good example would be a science park providing shared resources to other organisations located on its premises. These tend to be very innovative communities, committed to supporting each other's development.[13]

Direct Sales Model

Direct selling is marketing and selling products to consumers directly, away from a shop or a fixed retail location. Sales are typically made through party plan, one-to-one demonstrations, and other personal contact arrangements. So the business model focuses on a direct personal presentation or demonstration of the products and services to consumers, often in their homes or at their place of work.[14]

ACTIVITY 9 (cont.)

Franchise Model

Franchising is the practice of using another firm's successful business model. The franchisor (who owns the 'model') has a way or process or method of doing business that is highly effective and which he or she offers to share with franchisees (who in a sense lease the model). Thus the 'franchise' is an alternative to building 'chain stores' to distribute goods or services, and so avoids most of the investment and liability costs that would otherwise arise. Indeed, the franchisee takes the risk by investing in the model. However, the franchisor's success comes through the success of the franchisees. The franchisee is thought to be more motivated than an employee because he or she has a direct stake in the business.[15]

When you have reflected on what you think might support the business model and which motivators might be more problematic for it, go to the endnotes to see the suggested answers to these types of business models.

Summary

1. There are three essential personal benefits to being motivated, the 3 Es: energy, enthusiasm, and engagement.

2. There are three essential organisational benefits to having motivation in the workforce, the 3 Ps: performance, productivity, and, if the strategy is right, profitability.

3. Performance has three essential elements: direction, skills (including knowledge), and motivation.

4. In the workplace, since direction is established at senior level, performance comes down to two core elements: skill (and knowledge) and motivation.

5. There is a simple formula which is usually quite accurate in establishing what level one is performing at: this is $P = S \times M$, where Skills (S) and Motivation (M) are scored out of 10 and when multiplied together produce a percentage result.

6. The Pareto Principle, or 80–20 Rule, is a 4:1 ratio which indicates that there are four levels of motivation and four levels of

performance that are meaningful. We call these the four quadrants of performance.

7.   Nine ideas to boost productivity can be aligned with the nine motivators.

8.   Three primary ways of establishing or benchmarking productivity are through results monitoring, customer surveys, and employee appraisals.

9.   Different business models thrive best when aligned with the appropriate motivators.

Notes

[1]   A simple example of this distinction might be: few people would buy a car because it has air-bags, which are a feature; but many might buy the car if they know it is 'safe', which is a benefit of having the air-bag feature.

[2]   The etymology of enthusiasm bears this point out since it comes from the Greek *enthousiazein*, to be inspired or possessed by a god, or meaning 'god-breathed'; in other words, it seems to reflect some divine element of being, which of course is inherently attractive.

[3]   http://www.investorsinpeople.co.uk.

[4]   http://www.investorsinpeople.co.uk/the-journey: 'Organisations accredited against the Investors in People Standard report increased efficiency, improved engagement, better customer service and effective working cultures. 60% of Investors in People accredited businesses predict business growth compared to the UK establishment average of 47% (UKCES Employer Perspectives Survey, 2012).'

[5]   If the top 20% of employees produce 80% of the value and the remaining 80% of employees produce 20% of the value, then we have a situation whereby we have a ratio of 1 producing 4 units against 4 producing 1 unit; in other words, $4 \div \frac{1}{4} = 16$ times. More specifically, the top producers will produce 16 times more than the worst producers, and probably four times more than the average producer. This is highly significant, and it needs to be kept in mind that the bigger the organisation the stronger the Pareto Principle. Bigger numbers mean the harder it is to resist only 20% of your employees being truly productive.

[6] For example, a report by Oxford Economics in 2014 across five sectors (Retail, Legal, Accountancy, Media and Advertising, and IT and Tech) found that the average cost of replacing staff was £30,614 per employee, and that the overall financial impact of staff turnover across the five sectors analysed amounts to a staggering £4.13bn per year in the UK alone. How then to retain staff?

[7] Lou Adler, *Hire with Your Head: A Rational Way to Make a Gut Reaction*, New York: Wiley, 1998.

[8] Samuel Arbesman, *The Half-Life of Facts: Why Everything We Know Has an Expiration Date*, New York: Current, 2012.

[9] An often used example of this from the hard discipline of astronomy is that Pluto was designated as a planet up until quite recently; now apparently it is not a planet. If that can happen to a planet, imagine how much more fluid and changeable 'facts' about psychology, economics, and management might be.

[10] In the UK, the Marconi Company is a great example of a strong workforce let down by catastrophic leadership and a completely wrong and misguided strategy. Sir Ronald Grierson said of it: 'As destructions of shareholder value go, I cannot think of another case that even approaches this in dreadfulness.'

[11] Irving L. Janis, *Victims of Groupthink: A Psychological Study of Foreign-Policy Decisions and Fiascoes*, Boston, MA: Houghton Mifflin, 1972. The Bay of Pigs debacle is cited as a major instance of political groupthink.

[12] Rick Wartzman, GM: Lessons from the Alfred Sloan era, *Bloomberg Business*, 12 June 2009, citing Drucker's *The Effective Executive* (1967).

[13] Supportive might be: Friend, Creator, Expert, Searcher; problematic might be: Spirit, Star, Builder.

[14] Supportive might be: Builder, Star, Expert, Spirit; problematic might be: Defender, Creator, Director.

[15] Supportive might be: Defender, Expert, Builder, Director; problematic might be: Creator, Star, Spirit.

Chapter 6
Motivation and Teams

Everybody knows that teams are important because there is a relentless confirmation of this fact in the media, in education, and throughout organisational life. Our everyday expectations are that people should be 'team players', and the only exceptions to this are when we allow some maverick not to be because they have an astonishingly high level of ability or talent, and so become too valuable to lose. In sport it seems obvious that we need 'teams', and so too in business and organisations. The basic idea is that teams outperform. But outperform what or who?

Teams outperform groups – that is the essential distinction. But groups oftentimes are under the delusion or the groupthink that they are indeed teams. The key difference in terms of results is one of arithmetic. Groups just happen to be a bunch of people working together under a common denomination. For example, they may be called a 'department' like the administration or the marketing department. They may be called a 'faculty' like the maths or business school faculty. They may be called a 'unit', a 'branch', a 'section', a board, a committee, or governors, and so on. But in each case what we find is that they are just a bunch of people who happen to be together in a specialisation defined and needed by the organisation. The resultant arithmetic comes in when we consider how much energy does the group have?

ACTIVITY I

Consider the following questions:

How important is teamwork in your work?

How often do you conduct training programmes to ensure your team is effective, or how often do you experience such programmes?

How is the effectiveness of your team(s) reviewed?

How directly have you been involved in training programmes run by your direct line manager to ensure team building?

How many of your line managers review the effectiveness of their team(s)?

With a group of five people, then, the arithmetic means that they are arithmetically energised: 1+1+1+1+1 = 5. However, when a *team* of five is working the arithmetic is geometrical: 1×2×3×4×5 = 120. That is the power of teams versus groups. And it is why a team of average football players (or substitute your favourite team sport) can defeat a group of football players which contains some massively talented (but maverick) players. So team is an acronym for TEAM, which means Together Each Achieves More.[1]

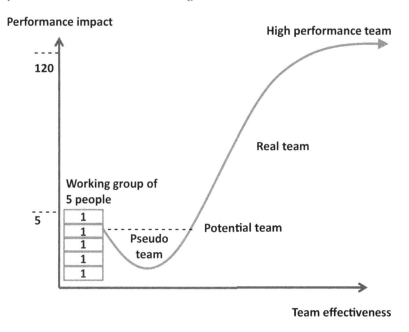

Figure 6.1   Developing a high-performance team

You notice in Figure 6.1 that we can go on building capability by simply adding numbers to our team, but it is far more effective to create the synergy along the line of the upward curve, which is the team energy. But this takes work – and there is a dip initially (where the 'pseudo' team emerges). And the dip is why so many abandon team building. 'It's not working', they say, and so they give up before they experience the benefits. There is a well-known formula that well expresses how the process of building a team works. First, there is 'forming'; then, as people clash to make sense of the process, there is 'storming', which produces the dip; but if we persist there is 'norming', where essential agreements and collaborations begin; and this finally gets us to 'performing', where the group is actually a team and starts achieving things. One additional point to make here is that although having gone through this process we may reach the altitude of a 'performing' team, we won't stay there for too long if there are no further inputs. Put another way, the 'performing' team will eventually become a 'conforming' group unless inputs revitalise it, in which case, if there are inputs, the 'performing' team becomes a 'transforming' team. This cycle clearly requires constant rejuvenation. In this sense it is exactly like motivation; it requires constant and persistent attention.

One clear mantra for all team leaders who genuinely want to lead teams and not manage groups is to pose this question whenever they encounter dysfunctional behaviour: 'Excuse me, Sam, are we a group or a team here?' And then watch the bafflement on their faces. Done often enough the word will get round the office or factory: 'What do you mean by that?' Having created mystery, perplexity, and curiosity, then use a team briefing to explain what you mean by the difference.

What, then, are the defining characteristics of a team? Let's be clear: there are many books containing many and multiple definitions. As always with Motivational Maps and its practitioners, we like the simple, the practical, and the relevant.

ACTIVITY 2

If a 'group' of people in a department, say, are effectively just a random collection of people who happen to have been put together ostensibly to work on some project or objective, what do you think might be the defining characteristics of a real team? List the core characteristics in your opinion. What do you notice about how real teams work?

There are at least four characteristics that are vital to creating effective teams.

First, the team has to have a clear remit, or mission. It is effectively what in military terms is called the Principle of the Objective.[2] It asks overtly, what do we exist to do or to achieve? This principle or question enables the focusing of all the energies in the team towards accomplishing the thing that is the most important, namely, the mission.

Second, teams have interdependency: the understanding that each person's gifts and abilities are needed to achieve the objective. Like a complex machine, all the parts fit and are necessary. But the corollary of this is that it is entirely possible to have redundant team members; their membership of the team is not essential to the outcome. This is bad. It means of course that the team is becoming less efficient – in fact, may be returning to becoming a group again. This may be viewed as an inevitable law of entropy. Things run down. There are many examples in corporates and the public sector where this waste and bloat is commonplace.

Third, there needs to be a belief that working as a team actually does produce better results than simply allowing individuals to do their 'thing' or perform at their highest level. This is a big belief that must never be taken for granted. It is important to assert in presenting this idea that thinking it is not the same as believing it. We frequently find managers and leaders who think this is true; but because they don't really believe it, then nothing substantial happens, and the group never transitions into a team.

Fourth, successful teams are accountable; this is really part of the remit. Having a remit means we know how well are we doing relative to achieving it. Great teams understand they are players in the bigger picture. They are accountable in two ways: they are accountable to each other; and they are accountable to the whole organisation to which they belong. This latter point is important for another reason too. Namely, the teams that are genuinely accountable tend not to create or develop fiefdoms: silos within the organisation that act as autonomous empires without responsibility to the bigger picture. For example, sales versus marketing, or HR versus operations, or senior managers versus middle managers, and so on. Such conflicts drain energy and resources and produce inefficiencies and ineffectiveness.

ACTIVITY 3

Review a team that you are a member of. How does it stack up in terms of the four criteria for effective teams, or is it just a group (called a 'department' for example) that you happen to belong to?

Score out of 10 your team's current position:

1. My team has a strong and clear remit or mission or purpose or objective ... /10.
2. My team needs the skills, knowledge, and personality of every member to achieve our remit or mission ... /10.
3. All the members of my team believe in the power of teamwork and are committed to working as a team ... /10.
4. My team is accountable to the whole organisation and we individually are accountable to each other for what we do ... /10.

(You might for question 4 want to score out of 5 for each of the two parts of the accountability question).

Where are you weak? Which scores are below 6 out of 10? What do you intend to do about it? One thing might be to ask all the group/team members to score these four questions too, and then compare results.

People want to be part of real teams, and scepticism and cynicism about teams is usually from individuals who have been deeply disappointed in their own experience of them. Like anything worthwhile, they are difficult to build and easily destroyed. But again, difficult maybe, but the value they produce for organisations can be out of all proportion to the difficulty of creating them.

ACTIVITY 4

Why do you think people want to be part of a real team? What is or are the attractions of it?

The person who has experienced real teamwork and been part of a team is always aware that something bigger than oneself is being achieved, which is why it feels so great. Indeed, being part of a real team can be considered one of life's greatest experiences: just under falling in love, great friendship (of which it can be a material part), and having children. Great teams create success in life as well as in achieving objectives, which is why Virgil 2,000 years ago observed: 'Success nourished them; they seemed to be able, and so they were able.' Some core part of our self is reinforced by effective teamwork and our self-efficacy rises, which is tantamount to saying that our self-esteem is boosted.

We need to constantly fine tune our teams because, as I said before, the law of entropy means they will run down without inputs. Here are nine tips then that will tune them or get you thinking about what you need to do to improve teamwork.

1.   Consistently and persistently talk to the team about what a team is, why it is not a group, and how it has geometric, not just arithmetic power. Raise your and their expectations of what is possible. Remember from Chapter 2 that expectations are core beliefs about future outcomes that affect our motivations and simultaneously can influence reality.

2.   Motivate yourself more to believe in teams. Here is a good reason: teams are important because you are not immortal – you will die, or retire, or resign, or transfer, or at some point leave the team/group of which you are member. At that point who takes over? Who succeeds? Teams ensure some genuine form of succession planning, and thus secure a legacy to the work that you have done. That's important isn't it? Groups, on the contrary, have little or no structure and so little of value can be perpetuated or transmitted to the future.

3.   Be certain that the remit or mission or objective is bold, big, clear, and compelling; be, like the Blues Brothers in the famous cult film, on a 'mission from God'! People want to be important, and what can be more important than doing something important with like-minded friends? For most people (and groups) work is an activity of which 80% or more is wasted time. Buy-in to clear, specific objectives is the antidote to this waste and the foundation of strong team performance.

4.   Understand that the two words 'team' and 'hierarchy' are mutually exclusive. You'll know that there's too much hierarchy in your organisation when you find everyone agrees with your views and deference is the norm. Groupthink beckons! It's not rank that decides what we do and how we do it, but relevance and contribution to the mission. Another way of expressing this is: if you are a leader, lay your ego aside and allow others to be big.

5.   Just as we speak of clarifying the objective, so we need to spend time negotiating roles in order to maximise each member's contribution, particularly by playing to their strengths and motivators. One good question is: 'how do I contribute to the objective?' And here's an even better one for the superior team: 'how can I contribute to the team?' People generally have more to give than we think; let's create the environment in which this potential can be released.

6.   Ensure you oil the machine. This follows from tip 5: a too rigid pursuit of objectives, of what I call the 'content', always leads to disintegration, as even the most powerful engine will burst apart if it is not oiled properly. 'Oiling', in team terms, is paying attention not just to the objectives but to the process. A favourite question I have for teams is: 'how do you interact with each other?' The answer speaks volumes, especially when it's something like: 'We don't'! Respect, liking and consideration for others in the team, works wonders when trying to achieve ambitious goals.

7.   Avoid blame and drive out fear. The driving out of fear is Point 8 of W.E. Deming's famous 14 Point programme for the transformation of management; and it was essential for him in terms of the whole organisational drive to achieve quality.[3] People will not give their best, or be creative, or solve pressing business problems if they feel that making a mistake is going to have dire consequences. Blame is

always destructive. We need therefore to stop doing it. If you are not sure whether you do it, ask – get feedback and act it on it rather than blaming the messengers. Be consistent in word and deed.

8.   Ensure accountability to the wider organisation. So far the tips have largely focused on getting the team in the right – the peak – condition to perform. But there is a danger: the silo effect, the fiefdom and empire-building scenarios wherein successful teams become detached from the wider organisation and exist to promote only themselves. This needs to be prevented at source by proper accountability, controls, and incentives. Just as the individual feels better and bigger as part of a functional team, so the team feels better and bigger as part of an organisation functioning fully and efficiently.

9.   Make sure you have fun – this can be easily overlooked or easily overindulged in. In the latter case, everything is fun but not much is being achieved, but this is the rarer phenomenon. The simple antidote to it is ensuring that fun follows achievement and becomes a form of ongoing celebration. But overlooking its importance and relevance is much more common: employees, even in good teams, sometimes have to find ways to amuse themselves at work because they are bored – there is little fun to be had, and work is deathly serious. This is a mistake and needs to be reversed.

If you take some of these ideas and run with them you will find they have a major impact on your teams, and thus on your productivity and profitability. Teamwork means teams work!

The ability to function effectively with others in a team is down to a number of factors, which include personality traits, attitudes, behaviours, and preferred roles; but one of the most important factors, often almost completely overlooked, is the motivational profile of the individual and of the individual compared with the team profile. This is really important because, as we have already established, motivation is about energy and the nine directions of energy. When you think about it, what could be more important for team achievement than the alignment of their energies with the mission? And, equally important almost, what could be more important than considering how the individuals' energies align or conflict? At root we are talking about the very capacity to perform – to move the car out of the garage as it were. This is the number one factor of all, surely.

With this in mind, then, mapping motivation is part of a bigger picture, the bigger picture of the team being able to achieve. And we need to consider each individual's profile as well as putting all their profiles together to consider what might be called a Motivational Team Map.[4] What does this mean, then, or what does it look like?

Figure 6.2   Nine motivators and Relationship, Achievement, Growth (RAG)

The motivators are in three groups of three (Figure 6.2). In general Relationship-type motivators conflict mostly with Growth-type motivators, and this is because at root Relationship motivators are slower, risk-averse, and change-resistant whereas Growth motivators are faster, risk-friendly, and change orientated (no value-judgement implied in these descriptors – context is critical for determining which are more relevant). Thus, we can outline their potential compatibility in the following way (Figure 6.3):

This grid is a simplification but it gives an overview of the principles. A full compatibility and non-compatibility chart available in the Motivational Team Map shows an even more detailed picture. Before studying it, however, you might want to reflect on how this works.

	Relationships	Achievement	Growth
Relationships			
Achievement			
Growth			

Very compatible ⬤   compatible ◯   potential tension ⬤

Figure 6.3   Simple motivational compatibility

ACTIVITY 5

You already know that that Growth and Relationship motivators tend to conflict. But consider all nine motivators. What other conflicts might there be? Take time to reflect on what each motivator wants, really wants:

Searcher wants to make a difference

Spirit wants to be autonomous

Creator wants to innovate

Expert wants to learn

Builder wants to be rich

Director wants control

Star wants recognition

Friend wants to belong

Defender wants security

For example, would you conclude that the Spirit and the Friend motivator align or conflict? Does the desire for autonomy square with the desire to belong? Is there alignment or conflict? Draw your own conclusions from the above list and then check your answers in Figure 6.4.

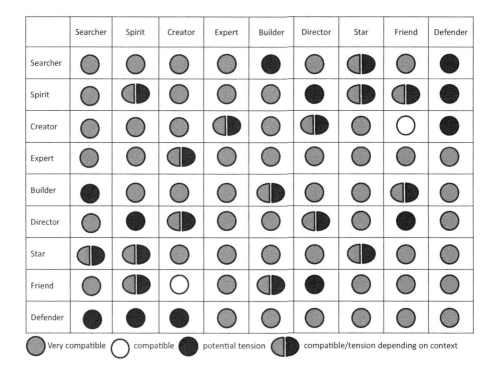

	Searcher	Spirit	Creator	Expert	Builder	Director	Star	Friend	Defender
Searcher	◑	◑	◑	◑	●	◑	◐	◑	●
Spirit	◑	◐	◑	◑	◑	●	◐	◐	●
Creator	◑	◑	◑	◐	◑	◐	◑	○	●
Expert	◑	◑	◐	◑	◑	◑	◑	◑	◑
Builder	●	◑	◑	◑	◐	◑	◑	◐	◑
Director	◑	●	◐	◑	◑	◐	◑	●	◑
Star	◐	◐	◑	◑	◑	◑	◐	◑	◑
Friend	◑	◐	○	◑	◐	●	◑	◑	◑
Defender	●	●	●	◑	◑	◑	◑	◑	◑

● Very compatible   ○ compatible   ● potential tension   ◐ compatible/tension depending on context

Figure 6.4   Complex motivational compatibility

We see, then, from Figure 6.4 that the desire for autonomy and the desire for belonging do indeed conflict; but it's not just these two. The desire for autonomy also conflicts with the desire for control. Of course it does: the more control we take on, the less freedom we have, and vice versa. This, interestingly (the combination of Director and Spirit motivators), is a regular feature in the top three motivators of Managing Directors in the UK: they are often torn between their desire to manage and their desire to be free of restraints. And this particular internal conflict has all sorts of consequences, one of them being a tendency, when it is unexamined by Managing Directors, for them to be perceived as inconsistent by their employees – they do not 'walk the talk'. Why and how? Because these two motivators will on the one hand lead them to micro-manage their employees (the Director) whilst at the same time actively resisting all constraints on their own freedom of movement (the Spirit). This is a classic anomaly and problem that using Motivational Maps can help resolve.

But now let's take this to another level; your top three motivators drive you to seek certain outcomes. Some of these motivators conflict; this can happen internally. For example, you may have Defender – the need for security as your top motivator – and it is equally scored with the Creator as your second motivator, the desire for change. You have in this situation an internal conflict in which the Defender in you wants stability, wants things to stay the same, and at the same time the Creator in you, almost as strongly, wants innovation, wants the new – and the result can be a kind of internal paralysis or indecisiveness: you do not know what you really want because you experience an internal feeling state that pulls you in two opposite directions.

If we consider this on the larger stage of a team, it should be clear that if you have a specific motivator as your primary drive, want, desire, and this is somebody else's lowest drive, want, desire – in fact so low it is almost an aversion – then we have within the group (if not an actual team) an opposition of energies (for that is what drives, wants, and desires are) which can lead to conflict or indecision or paralysis. Worst of all it can lead to conflicts which are subconscious in nature: we sense the opposition from someone else and we resent it. We think they don't like us or they are being difficult, and then our opposition to them kicks in. Funnily enough, if we do rationalise it, this opposition is often perceived to be a 'personality conflict'; more often than not, it is a motivational conflict.

Thus, for teams to grow and thrive they need to be aware of each other's motivational map or profile, and each member needs to be responsible, if only on a one-to-one level, for fuelling the motivators of other team members. What if that were possible because we could know that information and not just guess at it?

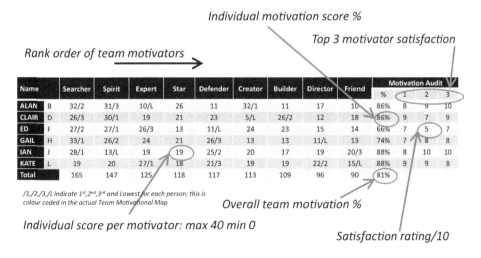

Figure 6.5   Anonymised team data table

Figure 6.5 shows an anonymised team data table. Six people in a team have all done a Map, and the results from this in a one-page Excel-type spreadsheet are revealed on page 22 of their Team Motivational Map. The actual map is colour coded, and I have here used numbering /1,/2,/3,/L to indicate a code for first, second, third, and lowest motivators. But notice the following obvious and useful information on the data table:

1.   The team is 81% motivated – a high level.

2.   The team really likes making a difference, autonomy and expertise.

3.   Alan B's very strong top motivator is also Claire D's very weak lowest motivator – there are other conflicts too.

ACTIVITY 6

Look carefully at Figure 6.5. What else do you notice about this team, either on an individual or on a team basis? Here are three specific things to pay attention to:
1.   Who has the lowest motivational score and why?
2.   Who else has highest v. lowest motivator potential conflicts?
3.   What might be the problem motivator in the top three for this to be a long-term fully functioning team?[5]

Further, just as the individual has a Personal Motivation Audit score – how motivated he or she is as a percentage – so these numbers aggregated can show what the motivational score is for the team. One metaphor for this might be: how much fuel is in the tank? Clearly, the higher the score the better: the more energy the team has (when focused), then the more likely it is that they will be productive for the greater good of the organisation.

Finally, it is important to realise that certain groupings of motivators within a team – the dominant pattern in fact – can have a massive relevance to fitness for purpose. Where, for example, we need speed in the workplace (operationally) or even in a sector (say, logistics), do we have a team whose motivators are predominantly slow? Alternatively, where we need thoroughness, accuracy, and care – which are slow in nature, since accuracy requires checking and double checking – do we have teams who are driven by the 'fast' motivators? There is not a right or wrong set of motivators here, any more than there is a right or wrong motivational profile for an individual; but what does drive the issue is context – what does this context require? That will determine the suitability of a profile.

If we look then at Figure 6.6 we see a short summary of which motivators are fast, medium, and slow, an issue we looked at in Chapter 4. This refers to speed in decision-making; but really this will be speed generally, since if the decision-making is slow there will tend to be a corresponding delay in implementation – not always, but usually. Clearly, teams can be purely in one category (in terms of their top three motivators) or the other, and they can be mixed as well. So there is plenty of complexity in this mix, but the principles are clear. Keep in mind, too, that fast speed also corresponds with risk and change friendliness, and slow betokens risk and change aversion.

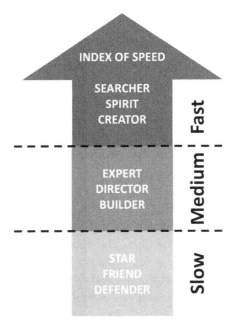

Figure 6.6   Index of speed

ACTIVITY 7

Given this account of the motivational profiles and the properties of the three types of motivator – fast, medium, and slow and so on – what might the characteristics be then of typical teams when:

a.   relationship motivators dominate
b.   achievement motivators dominate
c.   growth motivators dominate
d.   a mixture of all three types dominates?

Jot down your ideas on this before reading ahead.

When Relationship motivators dominate the team, then motivation comes primarily from feeling secure with others, belonging and friendship, and receiving recognition from each other. They will tend to be process and procedurally driven, loyal team players who value accuracy and doing things the right way. But also be mindful that because they like security and predictability they may shy away from taking risks and avoiding change. This can mean lost opportunities, and can effectively lead to a 'country club' atmosphere around work that may be underachieving. Could they perform at a higher level by approaching risk and change with a more positive attitude?

When Achievement motivators dominate the team, then motivation comes primarily from power and control, visible achievement and mastery. They will tend to be goal and results driven, competitive, and self-starters who value what works and effective outcomes. Be mindful that because they enjoy competition and achievement so much they may quickly burn out, as it can be all work and no play. This can lead to lost opportunities. Also, are they missing out on fulfilling relationships within the team, including the potential of teamwork itself? And further, the relentless pursuit of objectives can also drive out creativity and innovation.

When Growth motivators dominate the team, then motivation comes primarily from innovation and creativity, autonomy, mission, and making a difference. They will tend to be ideas and future driven, individualistic, and concerned with achieving their full potential and being all they can be. Be mindful that with such a growth and self-development focus they may fail to sustain necessary relationships and not be team players. Further, by focusing on mission, change, and being involved with new things, details are usually not their strong point, and they can initiate ideas and projects but sometimes fail to finish or follow through.

Finally, when no cluster is dominant then motivators are mixed in this team. In terms of the actual scoring this means that there is narrow range between all three types of motivator, no more than a 4% difference. Remember that context is everything: all combinations have their strengths – and weaknesses. In this case it may well be a strength in which a variety of motivators are effectively deployed through appropriate roles within the team. Alternatively, particular attention may need to be paid to each individual's motivators: to see, first, whether there are internal conflicts; and, secondly, whether there are any potential conflicts between individuals within the team. A warning sign that the motivational profile needs to be addressed would be that the team is indecisive or uncommitted, or even unfocused.

Another important aspect of the team map generally is what is called the Change Index. We have already established that the model is 'organic' and not 'discrete', by which we mean that all the motivators are not separate and disjointed concepts but indeed part of one whole: they are the nine motivational faces of what it means to be human. Just as the numbers in the Enneagram are all connected, so are the motivations; and this fact produces, as we already have seen with 'speed of decision-making', other properties that the Motivational Maps possess. Pre-eminent amongst these is the property demonstrating a predisposition towards change – and actually an attitude towards risk as well (for our purposes these two terms, change and risk, are virtually synonymous).

Built into the Team Motivational Map is a Change Index, calculated via an algorithm based on a weighting of the motivators, which seeks to establish how receptive a team is to change. Change is not good or bad in itself; but if big changes are necessary – and increasingly they seem to be – then whether or not a team is emotionally ready for or resistant to that change is an important factor to consider before implementation. It needs to be taken into account because even the best ideas will fail if the team motivationally or emotionally is not ready to accept them. And let us also be aware: teams that resist changes may have good reasons to do so, and may subsequently be proven right in their opposition – it was a bad idea.

ACTIVITY 8

Consider a team in which you have previously been a member: how change-friendly or change-averse were the team? How important was their attitude towards change in terms of the team achieving their remit? How might knowing or considering their attitude to change help in planning for success?

The score for the Change Index is a percentage which falls into four quadrants ranging from highly change-friendly to highly change-resistant (or averse). What we notice about this, however, is that another 'property' arises or correlates with the propensity to want change or to resist it. Namely, that those teams that actively seek change tend to be seeking effectiveness, whereas those teams that actively seek to resist change desire efficiency. Put another way: effectiveness teams will be concerned with outcomes, results, and faster speeds (people and things need to 'work'), whereas efficiency teams will be concerned with accuracy, detail, and slower speeds (people and things need to be 'right'). Again, neither is better or worse, but the context is decisive in deciding what kind of team we need in this situation. And keep in mind too: the more change resistant a team, the more resources we will need to make the change happen,[6] so this feeds into the planning process.

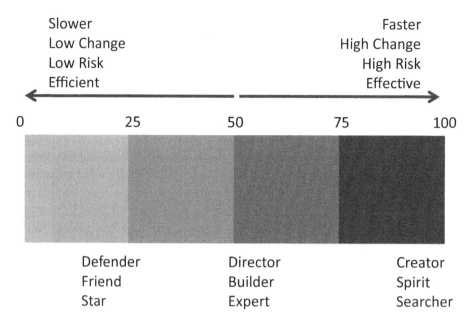

Slower		Faster
Low Change		High Change
Low Risk		High Risk
Efficient		Effective

Defender	Director	Creator
Friend	Builder	Spirit
Star	Expert	Searcher

Figure 6.7   Change/risk/speed/effectiveness/efficiency

Before considering the characteristics of a high-performing team, we need to mention that teamwork per se may not be the 'problem'. Poor performance can derive from a large number of factors that are not just team related.

ACTIVITY 9

Look closely at the following list and tick which ones you have encountered within organisations in which you have worked. Identify the three worst culprits and make notes on what their effects have been:

a.   poor recruitment and selection procedures
b.   confused organisational structure; ill-defined roles
c.   lack of proper controls and supervision
d.   poor training and development; personal stagnation
e.   lack of creativity and scant innovation
f.   inappropriate management philosophy, or none
g.   lack of succession planning or development
h.   unclear aims, objectives, and targets; failure to plan
i.   unfair rewards and recognition schemes, formally and informally
j.   little personal integrity and trust (essential for team development)

On top of these problems there is, of course, the problem that this book is addressing directly: low motivation and its consequent impact on morale, performance, and productivity.

So what then are the characteristics of high-performing teams? A list of 20 characteristics could easily be assembled, but for now let us consider nine really important ones. And while we are doing this, let us ask ourselves which of the motivators does this particular characteristic most comfortably sit or align with? In other words, which motivator wants to fulfil or realise this particular characteristic?

ACTIVITY 10

What do you think are the top three characteristics of high-performing teams? Which motivators do they most closely align with?

There needs, firstly, to be a shared sense of purpose and of vision that leads to a common understanding of what we are trying to achieve, and why. The motivator most engaged with trying to realise purpose and mission is the Searcher motivator; thus teams containing Searchers which do not have a clear purpose will seriously stress the members. Spirit, too, is relevant here as the Spirit motivator wants vision.

Second, high-performing teams need effective links with other teams as well as time spent looking for win-win advantages. This is quite entrepreneurial, and so the Spirit and Builder motivators are probably the most adaptable for these sorts of characteristic: the Spirit for the time flexibility, which they like, and the Builder because of the win-win deals that can lead to material advantages.

Third, high-performing teams thrive on useful and creative conflicts which take individuals beyond their comfort zone; alongside this there is a diversity of skills and backgrounds. This is tantamount to saying that such teams do not get stuck in the rut of routines, and also that they problem solve – and for that the Creator motivator is especially appropriate.

Fourth, there needs to be an enabling and encouraging of individual development for which resources may be required. Here the Expert and Star motivators may well feel at home.

Fifth, high-performing teams require appropriate leadership, one based on situation not hierarchy as we noted before. Here the Director motivator would like to step up to the plate to take control, whilst the Star likes being in the centre of things.

Sixth, high-performing teams like open communication with no hidden politics; direct, honest talk without fear of worry of consequences. These are characteristics that especially appeal to the Defender motivator, for whom clarity is a premium energiser.

Seventh, trust and mutuality, respect and understanding, and a sense of collective responsibility are essential characteristics of high-performing teams, and these qualities are most highly prized by the Friend motivator, as are the elements of fun and comradeship.

Eighth, high-performing teams like appropriate working methods to avoid wasting time, and consistently to have appropriate methods means regular review and reflection. The Searcher, Expert, Director, and Defender all want these characteristics.

Ninth, these teams celebrate success, and celebrating successes is something all motivational profiles enjoy. But add to this celebrating failure. Why? Because failures can indicate that we are not playing things too safe; we are stepping out of our comfort zones. Clearly, the high change motivators such as Searcher, Spirit, and Creator are here more likely to embrace this situation.

The key point underpinning these observations is that for a team to be successful and high performing it needs to be driven, and so specific motivators are more likely to drive certain aspects of the process that are commonly identified as being necessary for success. Overall it would appear that whilst certain projects benefit from specific motivational combinations, there is also a big benefit to be had in diversity where this contributes to the core processes underpinning high performance.

Summary

1.   Teams outperform groups because 'Together Each Achieves More'.

2.   Teams have four essential characteristics: mission, interdependency, belief, and accountability.

3.   Teams provide one of life's greatest experiences.

4.   Motivators in teams can conflict, as they can within an individual, and this can cause indecision, slowness of response, and confusion.

5. Generally speaking, Relationship-type motivators conflict with Growth-type motivators.

6. Motivators are correlated with speed of decision-making, change, risk, and even effectiveness and efficiency.

7. The Change Index of the Team Motivational Map seeks to indicate how responsive a team is to change or not; but responsiveness itself is not good or bad – it all depends on the context.

8. At least ten other factors, aside from motivation and teamwork, can cause performance problems in teams.

9. Motivators can usefully be aligned with the key characteristics of high-performing teams

Notes

[1] Apparently it can also stand for its direct opposite: Totally Engaged in Assisting Myself!

[2] Of the 12 Principles of Military Strategy, the principle of the objective is often said to be foundational, since without a clear objective no other strategy can effectively work.

[3] W. Edwards Deming, *Out of the Crisis*, Cambridge, MA: Massachusetts Institute of Technology, 1982; see also Rafael Aguayo, *Dr. Deming: The Man Who Taught the Japanese about Quality*. New York: Carol, 1990.

[4] See the Resources section at the end of the book for more information on the four different Motivational Maps that we produce, but these are: the Motivational (for individuals); the Motivational Team Map (for teams); the Motivational Organisation Map (for whole organisations); and the Motivational Youth Map for pupils at schools and colleges up to 18 years of age.

[5] Activity 5.1 – Ed and his Searcher motivator is not being fulfilled (5/10); 5.2 – Claire and Ed v. Ian, Kate v. Alan, and Alan v. Claire are the most prominent conflicts; 5.3 – the Spirit motivator may be problematic as the desire for independence tends to undermine the cohesion of the team, especially with Friend lowest overall.

[6] There are nine kinds of resources for change we need to consider: see Figure R.3 in the Resources section for a breakdown of all nine kinds of resources.

Chapter 7

Motivation and Appraisal

Performance Appraisal – or Employee Appraisal or simply appraisal – is a ubiquitous feature of modern management, and also of organisational systems. But what is it and what should it do?

ACTIVITY I

What is appraisal in your organisation? How does it work? How do you feel about it generally, and about your appraisals in particular: are they good or bad, useful or indifferent, valuable or time-wasting? What do they achieve? What are they supposed to accomplish? Jot down detailed answers to these questions.

Performance Appraisal is a subset of Performance Management, a topic too big to be dealt with here, except to say that Performance Management is the process by which an organisation ensures that its goals are being consistently met in an effective and efficient way. So Performance Appraisal is that part of the Performance Management process which enables management to ensure that individual employees are fitting in with organisational development over time. That development, of course, is most obviously apparent in its realisation of self-prescribed goals. In short, Performance Appraisal enables an alignment of people to strategic objectives and priorities, which will mean getting them to commit to certain goals.

The purpose of Performance Appraisal is really one thing and one thing only: to improve the employee's performance. All other purposes dilute this central mission and are correspondingly responsible for many of the reasons why Performance Appraisal fails to deliver. Gerry Randall describes it this way:

> Employee Appraisal can be seen as the formal process for collecting information from and about the staff of an organization for decision-making purposes … one overriding purpose of this decision making emerged, improving people's performance in their existing job.[1]

Performance Appraisal is essentially a twentieth-century phenomenon. The 'scientific' method – or Taylorism as it was called, after its founder, Frederick W. Taylor[2] – came to dominate industry at the start of the century; and as it did so there arose a corresponding problem whose solution appealed to the new and rising science of psychology, and in particular the work of William James. Taylorism, for all its simplistic appeal, ran into the problem of human productivity: you can stop-watch, time-manage, and 'specialise' everybody till your heart's content, but people have a curious way of not being productive, even though they are being paid to be so.

In short, it rapidly became apparent that for all the 'scientific' approach to management and productivity, and some gains made in certain areas, there was still a productivity shortfall. Further, this was down to employees not performing at high levels or at their best; and what was increasingly most noticeable about poor performance was that it was invariably correlated with poor motivation or lack of motivation.

Psychology enters the picture with the work of William James, who discovered three key principles of high performance.

ACTIVITY 2

What do you think are the three key principles of high performance? Reflect on times when you have performed at a high level, or consider somebody you know who definitely is a high performer. If it helps, consider a top-performing sports star who is known to perform. This can be useful since sport throws 'performance' into high relief. Jot down your answers before looking at William James' view.

So what are these solid psychological principles? William James discovered that people perform better when three essential conditions are met.

- First, that they are set clear goals and objectives. The importance of this cannot be overstated.[3] Basically, the goal or objective is the directional mechanism. It is what we are looking for and forward to; it gives us not only direction, but as it impacts our imaginations it stimulates energy, motivation, and enthusiasm. Notice, however, that linked with goals is the word 'clear' – many goals are vague and woolly. This can be fatal to their achievement or any success.

- Secondly, that they are involved in setting those goals and objectives. This is obvious when you think about it. For those who have young children, think back. You can stand towering above them and tell them what their 'objective' is in visiting Aunty Agatha – and then hope they behave! Or, you can kneel down at their level, talk at their level, and say a few things about what you hope will happen at Aunty Agatha's, and let them say what they hope will happen – and so go on to draw the threads together: what you both agree is going to happen at aunty Agatha's. This has much more chance of being effective. It might now technically be called empowerment: give people an input into the project ahead and you get buy-in.

- Finally, that they are given adequate feedback on how they are doing. Here, I must add: adequate is an 'inadequate' word to describe this process. People really perform better when they are given quality feedback – the kind of feedback where what they do is noted, its consequences articulated, praise is forthcoming, they are asked to repeat it, and confidence is expressed in them. In America they rightly call feedback 'the breakfast of champions'; and alongside this we need to consider William James' other profound and astonishing remark, that 'the deepest principle of human nature is the craving to be appreciated' – appreciation, of course, being a very specific kind of feedback.

This sounds simple enough, and almost an account of how the performance appraisal is supposed to work: managers meet employees in a one-to-one situation to discuss how they are doing; that is, to establish how well they are doing in achieving organisational goals. Plus, they then often provide 'adequate' feedback. This leads on to them, then, collaboratively setting new goals and objectives together. If they don't collaborate what would be the point of the meeting? They may as well email employees the goals. So, all very well in theory, but what about in practice?

ACTIVITY 3

Appraisal often has a bad reputation. What in your view are the problems and difficulties with it? Why does it fail to work? List as many reasons as you can and, where relevant, consider the specific issues in organisations in which you have worked. Finally, ask yourself this: if you had to choose one reason and one reason only why appraisal fails or fails to deliver performance enhancement what would that one reason be?

Appraisal is such a good idea, and it is founded on such solid psychological principles, that it is a wonder it has such a bad reputation, and that it fails so frequently to deliver. It was W.E. Deming, the great quality guru, who said that it took the average American six months to recover from Performance Appraisal.[4] The irony is not lost that the average American also experiences appraisals twice a year, so that in effect they never fully recover. Despite this, bosses complain that appraisal is ineffective, and employees complain it's all about ticking boxes. Why does it all go so badly wrong?

There are many reasons, but let's look at four. First, trying to implement appraisal systems in what might be termed a 'mechanistic' culture. Here hierarchies prevail, which means commitment is lacking. People expect to be told what to do, and bosses expect to know best, sometimes unintentionally (or not) even discounting the views of the employee. Thus the essential collaborative ingredient is always short-circuited. This of course is a violation of the core 'Together Each Achieves More' (TEAM) principle discussed in Chapter 6.

Next, job descriptions, whilst good in themselves, can be a source of tension set against notions of excellence. Excellence or outstanding performance often implies a beyond-contract arrangement. Employees then end up being judged on an expectation which is not in their job description. If this 'excellence' becomes the expectation, then the assessment is likely to be unfair. This in a way is a primary reason why appraisal can be seen to be a tick-box process: the ticking is against the criteria of the job description, which however may not allow for excellence, or alternatively demands it go beyond the original agreement and job definition. There is another issue too that arises from this job description problem which is not only about standards versus excellence but also of standards versus creativity. Appraisal is a system and, like any system, can become more or less flexible. A system which is too standard and target driven can easily become a drive for conformity. This can manifest itself at all levels: creating safe comfort zone activities; obsession with assessment measures and results; management groupthink, and so on. This drives out creativity and innovation – on which so much ultimately depends.

Another curious anomaly is also how appraisal might boost the individual performance but at the expense of the team performance. The drive to make the individual perform at a higher level can inflict damage on team morale, especially when the 'adequate' feedback becomes, as it often does, comparative: other team members are hitting targets ahead of you, so why aren't you, and so on. Once trust and confidence in the team goes, of course, the effect on individual performances is usually dire as disintegration overwhelms the team members, including those who are hitting targets.

Finally, there are the structural solutions for behavioural problems. Managers and bosses like this, since it appears, at least temporarily, that they are making progress. There is a performance issue which directly stems from the poor behaviour and attitudinal traits of the employees; this at the best of times is a difficult area to tackle. Sometimes, but not always, it is difficult for managers because the cause of the poor behaviours stems from poor management itself. Rather than contemplate *that* possibility, the bright idea is to create some structural change or introduce some new system which will dissolve the bad behaviour. The Romans observed this phenomenon some 2,000 years ago, for, as Petronius Arbiter observed:

> *We trained hard ... But it seemed that every time we were beginning to form up in teams we would be reorganised. I was to learn later in life that we tend to meet any new situation by reorganising, and a wonderful method it can be for creating the illusion of progress while producing confusion, inefficiency and demoralisation.*

So, rejigged structures and systems often (and to be fair, not always) fail to achieve any good result. In fact, appraisal as a system, even badly implemented, will only exacerbate bad behaviours. This is because the skills needed to conduct an effective appraisal are leadership skills, the absence of which have likely caused the problem in the first place, and so only provide another opportunity to demonstrate more ineptitude on the part of managers.

These are all very severe problems that impede the Performance Appraisal system from doings its 'job', namely, to improve individual performances. It must be stressed as well that the above 'four plus' points are not exhaustive: there are many other problems too with Performance Appraisal. But if I had to choose one, perhaps the most obvious and significant is the quality of the manager, or the leader, or the one who is the appraiser: the one who does the appraising. Indeed, to speak anecdotally, in my own experience of having gone into hundreds of organisations to work with employees and managers and run management development training programmes, I find again and again that employees can put up with all sorts of appraisal problems: lack of resources (a private space, for example, even to conduct the meeting), poor documentation, lack of time, poor structure or ineffective systems, wrong attitudes, rating errors, lack of senior management commitment, and so on. But what they cannot forgive is the 'pointless encounter'. And we all know what this means:

we are supposed to be meeting our superior in order to get some quality feedback (some help in fact) on how we are doing, and maybe some boost, some motivation, to continue doing it – and we get nothing at all. Sometimes, and indeed often, we get demotivated, and the person who is being paid more than us has just wasted at least one hour of our time (two or three if we add in our preparation time and follow-up) and dashed our expectations. Somehow we – the employee – just never seem important enough to spend time with.

In other words, the most serious cause of discontent and demotivation in the appraisal process stems from the inadequacy of the appraiser; and organisations know this because that is why they spend huge amounts of money – billions in fact – training appraisers on how to conduct an appraisal interview. The primary focus of such training is 'soft skills' of the Emotional Intelligence or Neuro-Linguistic Programming or 'how to win friends and influence people' variety.

ACTIVITY 4

What soft skills or communication skills training have you received? Is it effective and has it helped you in your work as a leader or as a team member? What problems or issues can arise as a result of soft skills training in your experience?

'Soft skills' training is good, so far as it goes, but there are two major problems with it in connection with performance appraisal. The first, and most intractable, is that no amount of knowledge or insight, even coupled with relevant skills, is going to enable a manager or boss to run a good appraisal programme when they personally are – what might be called – 'psychologically or emotionally deficient'. By this I mean that the manager is using their position to play games that derive from their own inner negativity.

This might be summed up as having, in Transactional Analysis terms,[5] one of three negative life positions:[6] first, 'I'm OK, you're not OK', which will lead them to consistently 'put down' the subordinate. Or, 'I'm not OK, you're OK', in which they will lack confidence for positive follow-through; or worst of all, 'I'm not OK, you're not OK', which leads to despair and cynicism and the self-fulfilling prophecy of hopelessness – what's the point, nothing works, does it? If, as a boss or manager, these sound like familiar attitudes in those below (or even above) you, then the best advice is to try to develop a strategy for dealing with it before attempting appraisal. Appraisal will only expose the glaring deficiencies, not remedy them. Training, clearly, is not the answer.[7] However, whilst this is commonplace generally, in the best organisations it is

LIFE POSITIONS

Figure 7.1   Four life positions

the exception; for most people there, most managers and leaders actually want to do a good job, but they can't because …

Secondly, where training is the answer, the appraiser receives relevant soft skills training[8] and they develop (in two words) 'communication skills', there is a further problem: they usually cannot develop them at a sufficiently deep level, particularly when compared with consultants, trainers, and coaches who go in afterwards to try to resolve the ongoing issues. This is because acquiring skill sets at a deep level is not a question of going on a one-day or two-day or one-week course. It's reckoned that it takes something like at least 21 days to embed a new skill;[9] and keep in mind that these sorts of skills, dealing with ambiguity as they do, are not the easiest to master. Organisations on the whole simply can't afford to train staff to that level of expertise (especially in what is seen as a non-mission critical aspect of the business) and employees do not have the motivation to want to acquire that level of skill because it is usually not core, as they perceive it, to their job performance (and not correspondingly targeted or rewarded either). And this directly generates a third problem: those who are trained in soft skills find that their efforts to appraise effectively are undermined by the perceptions of the employees they begin appraising.

This last phenomenon is particularly obnoxious, and it stems from this fact: whilst employees love training that impacts suppliers and customers – say, for example, negotiation or customer service skills – they are more wary of training that impacts them. That is, they are wary – they dislike – management training. Hence the typical and sardonic comments of employees about managers (when they are attempting appraisals) that they have 'just been on a course', or this is some 'bright idea', meaning usually a very dim one. Nobody wants management stuff done to them, and so the only way of doing it is so that it appears to be natural. Natural here equals authentic and genuine. In other words, the only way to be effective is by way of having deep learning, so that the skills seem effortless and automatic. The analogy might be with a great actor or actress: the best never seem like themselves, but always like the characters they are playing – but to be natural or genuine in a role requires massive amounts of practice, and it is only then that we can fully suspend our disbelief in the action and the characters and fully engage with what is happening. Warren Bennis expressed it this way: 'Being genuine is the key factor of leadership.'

We come, then, to a crux problem: in most organisations in the commercial and public sector world the appraisal process has a demotivating effect on employees, and consequently erodes performance.[10] Ultimately it becomes another reason why the employee leaves the organisation prematurely and takes their knowledge and expertise with them. So the question becomes: is there a way that we can improve the one-to-one process when appraiser and employee meet, which is core to making the whole thing work? Clearly, training on 'communication skills', whilst good, is not the whole solution, as it can never be enough. What to do, then?

As a sidebar, one way round the problem is said to be 360° appraisal whereby the employee is appraised not only by the line manager but also by peers, subordinates, and possibly other super-ordinates. Great claims are made for this process, and it does often eradicate rating errors and intentional distortions, because so many are involved that discrepancies are evened out. But because so many are involved, it is very expensive, very time-consuming, and indeed bureaucratic;[11] and there is one other fatal aspect to its widespread adoption: namely, it weakens management. Managers are paid to manage, to make tough decisions, and to say it as it is; what 360° allows is for others to do the manager's job for him or her. They need never pull anybody up over their performance, since they can wait till appraisal time to get others to 'stick the knife in'. And of course, whilst 360° has the potential to eradicate unfair ratings, it equally has the potential to allow scores to be settled and personal agendas to percolate through the paperwork haze. Finally, 360° does not move away from the central problem of being in think mode, only now we have a whole bunch of people 'thinking' about one employee's performance; is this good?

If 360° is not the solution, what is? It is here that Motivational Maps has an astonishing ability to reframe the problem. First, though, let's delve a little more deeply into it. Schultz and Schultz note that:

> *employees that will be directly affected by the Performance Appraisals are less than enthusiastic about participating in them ... and that when an employee knows that their work performance has been less than perfect it's nerve racking to be evaluated. Most workers just don't appreciate constructive criticism or any criticism. Employees tend to be hostile knowing they could be given bad news on their performance.*[12]

Indeed! In fact when we think about it, who really does like so-called 'constructive criticism', whether it be at work or anywhere else? Not many people.

The problem, reframed, is that we are all fearful of so-called constructive criticism, especially when most of the time the criticism is not even constructive; and that is the typical experience of the average employee. What soft or communication skills are attempting to do is make the criticism palatable, acceptable, and at the very least not counterproductive.

But what causes the fear? This is the central issue because what causes the fear is responsible for the shutdown in creativity, in commitment, in energy, in engagement that leads to sub-par or mediocre performance, and fading motivation.

ACTIVITY 5

Consider both Performance Appraisals that you have experienced (or even delivered) and situations when you have been on the receiving end of 'constructive criticism'. How did you feel? What emotions went through you as the process progressed? How did you cope with these emotions? Specifically, did you experience fear or anger or guilt, the three most typical negative emotions?

What causes your fear? And how would you recommend coping with it or obviating it? How can Performance Appraisal interviews not generate fear?

The reason why employees and people generally experience fear when they are being reviewed is primary: it is because they are in Think mode, and in Think mode we can be wrong. We met 'Think' in Chapter 3 when we discussed the properties of Feel-Think-Know. Here the important extra point to understand is that nobody wants to be wrong; but that is the opportunity that Thinking provides us with. Being wrong, of course, has a profound impact on our self-image, that old friend we met in Chapter 2. So we need a detour to explain more fully what we mean by this and how it relates to motivation and Motivational Maps.

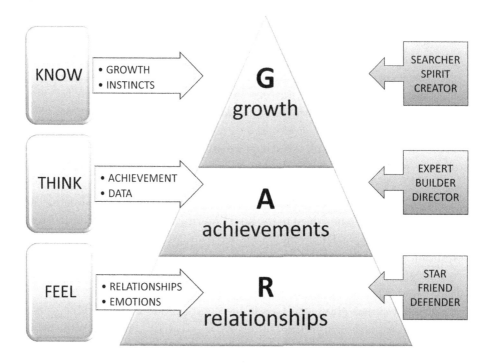

Figure 7.2   Feel, Think, Know and motivators and RAG

We see when we look at Figure 7.2 that we meet again the three primary modes of perception, but now matched alongside the nine motivators and the three elements: we feel, we think, and we know; and they are quite distinct within us, and each one has different properties. Another word for properties might be strengths and weaknesses; and the truth is that in the perfect human being these three modes of perception would be aligned and would be in balance. But, as I said, in the perfect human being ...

Given this, it should perhaps be clearer why Think generates fear and that, by way of contrast, Feel and Know do not. Why, we will discuss shortly; but for now suppose we could have a Performance Appraisal system that enabled us to bypass the Think at a critical moment, and thereby the fear. That supposition was effectively the promise of soft skills training, a promise that does not usually materialise because the soft skills were not embedded deeply enough. Appraisers tended to end up 'small talking' their employees with 'How's the wife? How's the husband? How are your kids?'[13] as a way of building rapport before plunging in with the performance knife: 'I see you didn't reach you numbers this quarter.' This clearly doesn't work, for the employee rapidly sees that a technique is being used on them, and we are too quickly back and onto judging them and their performance.

But Motivational Maps takes a different course by structuring a process that incorporates Feel, Think, and Know (Figure 7.3).

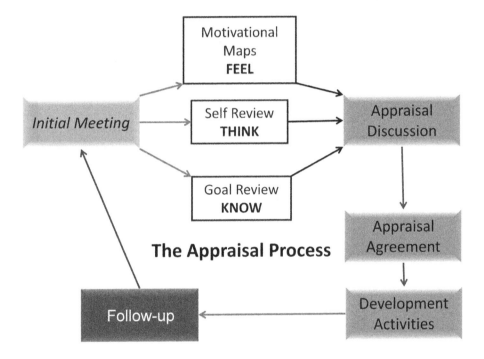

Figure 7.3   Appraisal process flow chart

And a number of points need to be made about Figure 7.3. The central issue is managing the one-to-one conversation so that it is natural, authentic, and genuine. To this end, firstly, then, consider the conversation as occurring in three parts, and that each part of the conversation has a dominant communication mode. We don't start with Think (we bypass it), because we know that it produces fear. Instead we start with Feel, because the great thing about feeling states is that they can never be wrong. Your feeling state is you;

if you feel angry or feel sad it may not be the most helpful thing for you, but it is not wrong: it is how you are at that moment. And here's the thing: to say to another person that you are wrong to feel some emotion is tantamount to denying them as a person. Thus, to use an example, if one said to one's boss 'what you did was crass and stupid', then that might be grounds for rebuke even if the assertion were correct. 'You think I am crass and stupid but you are wrong', the boss retorts (along with 'you're fired'!). But if you said, 'I felt angry when you did that', what could the boss say except, at best, 'I am sorry you felt that way.' Thus working at a feeling level and in the Feeling mode is quite a different experience from working in the Thinking mode; and we need to be definite and re-emphasise here that we always default to Think mode because we are rushing to judge how our subordinate performs.

So before we go any further, let's be really clear about what the purpose of Performance Appraisal is and what its core objectives ought to be. And, in stating this, I am also saying that all add-ons to these criteria will substantially weaken – dilute – the process; it needs to be focused and defined. Earlier I asked whether having lots of employees thinking about an individual's performance via 360° was good, and the reason I did so was to address this issue of what Performance Appraisal was really for.

The central purpose of Performance Appraisal is to improve performance; that's it![14] But from that definition stem three strong objectives that all appraisers need to bear in mind if they are going to be successful. These three objectives are:

1. to review past performance (past)

2. to motivate the employee (present)

3. to set targets for new performance levels (future).

You will remember in Chapter 2 that we outlined how the three primary sources of motivation had past-present-future perspectives. So here too we look back on how the employee has performed in the past (that may be the last three or six or 12 months), and whilst we are doing that it is vital that we sustain the employee's motivation in the present; in other words, it becomes a requirement of conducting a Performance Appraisal that the appraiser motivates the employee. Usually it is assumed that the mere act of conducting some formal review will have that effect, but it should be obvious from all that we have covered, including W.E. Deming's observation on Performance Appraisal in America, that this is not the case. Finally, after we have covered the two bases of the Past and Present we can move on to the Future – the thing that is really important in fact, for when you think about it, it's all very well assessing how they've done, but it's more important to consider what they are going to do; the former is fixed, whereas the latter is malleable. As the great ice hockey player Wayne Gretzky put it, 'A good hockey player plays where the puck is. A great hockey player plays where the puck is going to be.'

The word 'finally' in the last paragraph has special resonance and meaning here – finally! What I am getting at is that we all rush to judgement, and that we are better off if we don't, and if we leave it till 'finally' rather than 'firstly'. If we focus on the motivation first, if we focus on the Feel state first, then we have far more chance of achieving our objective, which is to set great new targets in which there is employee buy-in, commitment, and engagement – which will lead to enhanced performance. Put another way, the Motivational Maps approach defers the gratification of rushing to judgement and lets it emerge as leaves emerge from a tree; when that happens the process has life in it and begins to make a difference to how the employee feels and so what they subsequently do.

So to return to the model, Figure 7.3, we see that although we have talked about Past-Present-Future in that order, we need to structure the appraisal discussion so that the Present comes first, so that we motivate the employee. To do that, then, we use their Motivational Map as a basis for the discussion. Why? Because the Motivational Map describes but does not judge feeling states;[15] all motivators are equal, and having a low motivation does not always or necessarily correlate with low performance levels. Employees can, by act of will, perform at a high level although their motivation level is low, as we mentioned in Chapter 1. Besides, low motivation at work is often and self-evidently not the employee's fault, and managers know that. On day one of a new job employees are most often highly motivated, so we know that the process of being at work causes motivational levels to deteriorate. It is a primary responsibility of managers and leaders to motivate employees, but as often as not they don't see it that way – and certainly don't do it.

If we consider the appraisal discussion to take one hour (maximum, but 40 minutes is even better), then the structure of it needs to be, say: 20 minutes reviewing the employee's Motivational Map (Feel mode); 20 minutes reviewing the employee's self-review (Think mode but now directed at their own self-assessment rather than directly at how they performed with organisational goals); and finally 20 minutes setting targets for future development (Know mode).

ACTIVITY 6

Review your own experience as an appraiser and as someone being appraised. Reflect on your appraisal interview, how much time was allocated to it, and how that time was segmented. What proportion of the time, do you think, was spent motivating you or did you spend motivating the employee? What proportion was spent on allowing the employee's self-review? And finally, what proportion was spent on reviewing past performance? In the light of what has been said, can these proportions be improved? What needs more time, what needs less, and what have you got about right?

It may seem odd, possibly inexplicable, why I have described the final stage of the appraisal discussion as in Know mode, especially when we consider that this is the part of the conversation that is really of relevance to the organisation: how have you done and what are you going to do? If Know mode is all about intuition and gut instinct, then that hardly seems the methodology to dictate the correct way forward. And that is a good point; but we need to understand how people work rather than how rigid processes achieve 'quality', but often no result.

The truth is that once you engage employees (or anybody) at a Feel level, then they start resonating with you, or begin to feel that you are on their 'wavelength'.[16] What this means is that they become more excited, more energised (more motivated), more open, more committed, and more engaged; they can't help themselves. Add to this that the Map is doing this, not the manager's often insufficient soft skills. In other words, there is no pretence in using the Motivational Maps that I am interested in you personally; instead, you, the employee, have completed an extremely interesting self-assessment tool and I, as your manager, want to talk about it with you. More specifically, I want you, the employee, to talk about it to me because I have a few questions I want to ask you about it. This raises the professional game. Given that start, any manager (apart from the truly disturbed or profoundly thoughtless, which in reality constitutes a very, very small minority) can get a result. There is nothing disingenuous about asking an employee about their Motivational Map in the way that there is when a manager uses their soft skills to 'soften' up an employee. The former is part of the job; the latter is often perceived as manipulation – the employee being 'done' by management.

What, then, are the few questions that we want to ask that might lead to insight and engagement? It should come as no surprise that I don't recommend using any set of questions mechanically since one tends to get mechanical answers; but these 10 questions I have found to be highly effective, usually by selecting four or five of them as the basis for the conversation (Figure 7.4). Bear in mind, we are not trying here – as we might in a coaching situation – to exhaustively analyse the meaning for the Mapper, but rather to get their buy-in to what the Motivational Map is saying about their motivators and where that takes us in future and by way of alignment – alignment here meaning, where possible, that the targets that will eventually be set do in fact have aspects within them of meeting the employee's motivational profile.

How did you find your Map? Or, what did you think of your Map?	Does your current role fulfil your three Motivations? Why? How? Why Not? How Not?
How accurate was your Map?	How can you get more motivated?
How useful was your Map?	How can I enhance your current role?
What did you learn from your Map?	How can the organization help you enhance your motivation?
What will you do differently as a result of your Map?	How can you support and help motivate other employees? And specifically, employees in your team?

Figure 7.4   10 questions on completing a Motivational Map

ACTIVITY 7

You were invited to do a Motivational Map in Chapter 4. Assuming you have completed this and got your 15-page Map report – and if not please do this now – review the 10 questions and select five that you would ask yourself. Jot down your answers. What do you learn about yourself or your capabilities from such a review?

Clive Fletcher observed: 'If Performance Appraisal is to be constructive and useful, there has to be something in it for the participants – both the appraisers and appraisees [employees].'[17] It should be clear already that the Motivational Map provides something constructive and useful for both the appraiser and the employee; the conversation is off to a positive and flying start. We are not treating people as characterless 'units of production'; we are seeking to understand their motivations and talents, and to address those motivations, as well as to deploy their talents. The net result when we ask question 10 – 'How can you support and help motivate other employees? And, specifically, support employees in your team?' – is that we are beginning the process of building a high-performance team in which each member is starting to support others.

Having established, then, what motivated the employee, with the emphasis on the employee having established it, the appraiser can move onto the rest of the appraisal discussion. This area we will cover more briefly as it should be more familiar. But the next stage is shifting from Feel – how the employee feels about their Motivational Map – to Think, their own self-review. Self-review increases the effectiveness of the appraisal process, but it should be obvious that it does so since it is an indirect aspect of William James's formula for driving performance: namely, asking an employee to self-review before the appraisal discussion is involving them, albeit at a preliminary stage, in the formulation of their own new targets.

There are many ways to conduct a self-review, and no one right way, but here are five excellent questions that get to the core of how we are doing in a non-judgemental way.

5 Key Self-Review Questions	Notes to Consider
What am I most proud of accomplishing recently? Why?	Can you think of 3 specific things and which one's top?
What tasks/projects have proved most difficult? Why?	Lack of money, expertise, resources, support? What?
What do I hope to achieve over the next six months?	How build on what I have already achieved?
What changes have happened in the last 6 months?	Technical, customer, management, team, environmental, personal...?
Do we need to review my job description?	Does my job description reflect what I do and am I being assessed on it or on something else?

Figure 7.5   Five self-review questions

Finally, we need to move to the third stage of the appraisal discussion, where we are in Know mode; here we review the actual performance – or the outcomes that were set last time – and we use that as the basis for the next round. A good metaphor would be that it's rather like sailing. Last time we

> ## ACTIVITY 8
>
> Look back at your work and performance over the last six or 12 months; ask yourself these five questions and make notes on your answers. What do you need to do as a result of these reflections? Make an action plan.

set off from the shore with a clear sense of direction; after a period of time we have reached point A, but we now need to take our bearings and correct our course if we want to arrive in the port that is our destination. But here's the thing: having established what motivates our employee in a non-threatening or fearful way, then having established what they think about what they are doing and how they are performing, how much easier is it going to be to get agreement on what needs to happen next? No methodology with people is going to get a 100% response, because people are people and, as we established in Chapter 1, there is an ambiguity about them and their responses which is problematic, especially for those people who demand certainty. But what this does is increase the odds of success massively in favour of the appraiser, and hence of the organisation.

Now we can say, 'How have you done?' We can itemise performance against targets and we are likely to find out what has really happened, whether we actually know or not. Alongside this it is also important to allow the employee to inform us of what factors may have blocked or prevented him or her from achieving targets; we ask them to reflect on it anyway in their self-review, so let's find out. It may be something important that we can improve. Surely, shouldn't this be a primary reason why we talk to employees, to find out what is really going on?

> ## ACTIVITY 9
>
> Consider your own work or role. What factors have blocked you from performing at a high level or from achieving targets? Here are six areas to consider:
>
> 1. Personal factors (including motivational ones)?
> 2. Skill and knowledge factors?
> 3. Managerial factors?
> 4. Team factors?
> 5. Environmental factors?
> 6. System factors?
>
> What can you do personally to unblock any of these blockages? Whose help do you need to enlist to help you break through any one of these blockages? What blockages cannot realistically be removed? What, then, needs to happen – for example, do targets need changing?

I have now covered a lot of ground, and it should be clear how Motivational Maps with their alignment with Feel, Think, and Know can provide a radical new approach to the most problematic area of the Performance Appraisal system: namely, the one-to-one discussion itself. The chapter has outlined the key principles as well as providing some useful materials to adopt; and adopt is an important word, since all organisations are different. My final comment on it for now is that off-the-shelf solutions to Performance Appraisal problems are not likely to work. Instead, these key principles and ideas that I have outlined need to be adopted and incorporated into existing systems, and that is usually not only not impossible, but extremely do-able with proper foresight and planning.

Summary

1.   Performance Appraisal is ubiquitous in organisations but poorly executed.

2.   William James discovered three key principles of high performance: goal setting, involvement in setting goals, and 'adequate' feedback on progress.

3.   Despite Performance Appraisal replicating James' principles, appraisals fail for a variety of reasons, including hierarchical structures and structural solutions for behavioural problems.

4.   Most importantly, appraisals fail because managers are either psychologically compromised or have insufficient soft skills to persuade employees that the interview is meaningful.

5.   Employees fear being wrong.

6.   Motivational Maps reframes and recasts the appraisal discussion.

7.   Each appraisal discussion should be in three parts, reflecting the three Feel, Think, and Know elements of human communication.

8.   Using the Motivational Map initially in the interview to discuss Feel states is non-judgemental and supportive.

9.   Deferring judgement of performance till the end of the interview allows for agreement and mutuality in deciding the way forward.

Notes

1   Gerry Randell, Appraisal, in Keith Sisson (ed.), *Personnel Management in Britain*, Oxford: Blackwell, 1989.

2   Definition of Taylorism: 'a factory management system developed in the late 19th century to increase efficiency by evaluating every step in a manufacturing process and breaking down production into specialized repetitive tasks' – Merriam-Webster Dictionary.

3   We have already met this issue in several guises, but for instance see endnote 2 in Chapter 6, where the principle of the objective is crucial to military strategy.

4   Derek Torrington and Laura Hall, Personnel Management: HRM in Action, London: Prentice Hall, 1995; also, see Tom Peters, Appraising employees: There are no sure-fire rules, *Chicago Tribune*, 28 October 1985.

5   Thomas A. Harris, *I'm OK, You're OK: A Practical Guide to Transactional Analysis*, New York: Harper and Row, 1969.

6   Of course the fourth position – I'm OK, You're OK – is the healthy, assertive position.

7   What is the answer then? The reality is that co-dependent, game-playing people need something much stronger than training, and even than coaching: they need therapy or counselling, and this is highly labour-intensive, expensive, and not guaranteed to work. One has to consider the damage that they do set beside the value they contribute to the organisation, and effectively a cost-benefit analysis as to whether they should be retained.

8   The link between employee appraisal and interpersonal skills is advocated by Sashkin, who insists that not only are such skills necessary for effective delivery of Performance Appraisal but they are also central to long-term sound management practice – see Marshall Sashkin, *Assessing Performance Appraisal*, San Diego: University Associates, 1981.

9   Maxwell Maltz, *Psycho-Cybernetics: A New Way to Get More Living out of Life*, Englewood Cliffs: Prentice-Hall, 1960; but more recent research by Phillippa Lally, a health psychology researcher at University College London, and colleagues in a study published in the *European Journal of Social Psychology*, suggests that at least 66 days is necessary and sometimes much longer. See P. Lally, C.H.M. van Jaarsveld, H.W.W. Potts, and J. Wardle, How are habits formed: Modelling habit formation in the real world, *European Journal of Social Psychology* 40/6 (2010): 998–1009.

10 Appraisals fail to motivate employees, says a survey by employee assessment consultants Saville and Holdsworth (SHL), and almost 50% of respondents to an Industrial Society survey

claim that appraisals have no positive effect on the workforce. 'Some 90% of respondents to our survey cited employee motivation as one of the main objectives of an appraisal process', explains Roy Davis, Communications Manager at SHL. 'Despite this, not a single survey respondent stated that appraisal was a very good way of doing this.' – Performance appraisal systems could do better, *Management Today*, 1 April 1998. Or, 'few people report that they are satisfied with the way it [PA] is done in their organization' – Andrew M. Stewart, Performance appraisal, in Dorothy M. Stewart (ed.), *Handbook of Management Skills*, Aldershot: Gower, 1987.

[11] 'but there are problems: a minimum of 8 people commenting on 15 managers means at least 120 forms – a significant increase in administration; many appraisers found it difficult to comment on the individual manager's objectives; and there was a reluctance to back up ratings with anecdotal comments'. – Mike Thatcher, Appraisal, *People Management*, 21 March 1996.

[12] Duane P. Schultz and Sydney Ellen Schultz. *Psychology and Work Today* (10th, International edn). Upper Saddle River, NJ: Pearson Education, 2009, pp. 108–9.

[13] 'Indeed it will positively help if you are conversant with the jobholder's hobby, interests or family life. Show genuine interest.' – quoted in Clive Fletcher, *Appraisal: Routes to Improved Performance*, London: Institute of Personnel and Development (IPM), 1993.

[14] There are at least seven great and seemingly valid distractions that hijack a real Performance Appraisal performance conversation. Here they are with a brief explanation:

Evaluation: how well are we doing the job?
Auditing: what jobs are being done?
Succession Planning: who should be promoted?
Training: what do people need to do the job?
Controlling: I am telling you what to do.
Development: I/We are looking forward to plan.
Validation: I/We know the right things are being done.

[15] I need perhaps to comment on the fact that the Motivational Map is a Think tool in that it has been constructed in a deliberate and systematic way; but that does not mean it cannot be used to elicit Feel, and even Know, states.

[16] There is a wonderful phrase from Thomas Fuller: 'Seeing's believing, but feeling's the truth.'

[17] Fletcher, *Appraisal: Routes to Improved Performance*.

Chapter 8

Leadership, Motivation, and Engagement

If we consider the number one factor that affects organisational success, and if we were writing a book that focused on motivation at the same time, we might like to conveniently conclude that motivation was the single most important component of it. But that would be wrong. Clearly, not just one thing is responsible for high achievement and big success; there is a synergy in which several strands all work together to make the magic work.

ACTIVITY I

What do you think are the core components of organisational success? Make a list of at least six items and then prioritise them. When you have reviewed your own list what do you consider to be the single most important factor contributing to organisational success?

Some great ideas that you may have come up with that contribute are:

- having clear goals together with a flexible plan;

- focusing whole organisational strength on the key issue;

- taking the offensive in the marketplace and sustaining it;

- finding your competition's weakness and exploiting it;

- anticipating competitors' plans and concealing one's response;

- ensuring all employees are engaged and there is total commitment.

These are all powerful ideas which, if pursued relentlessly, can make a major impact on one's chances of success, but they are not the single most important factors. They are either strategic or people issues (though I would argue people are a strategic issue). But it should come as no surprise to learn that the single most important factor is in fact the quality of leadership – and the quality of the leader. In other words, and regrettably for all those who want to make business and organisational life a 'science' (remember Taylorism in Chapter 7), the ambiguous, the difficult, and the unpredictable human factor.

There need really be no academic proof for this assertion that leadership is the number one factor, for any cursory consideration of reality shows it to be true.[1] In the first instance from observing the difference a great leader makes who takes over from a weak one – whether we are talking education, the public sector, business, military, or politics – the result is the same: one person in a seemingly impossible situation that others have wholly failed to address seems to be able to rise triumphant and turn things round. A classic book in this field is Norman F. Dixon's which, whilst confining itself to the military field, draws the conclusion that psychologically healthy leadership makes all the difference in the world to outcomes, which in military terms is a matter of life and death, and indeed of the survival of whole civilisations.[2] But when we look at organisational life itself we find that researchers going right back to the 1950s found the wrong kind of leadership expressed in psychological terms:

> There can be little doubt that the major problem in industry today is the problem of suitable leadership. There are far too many petty Hitlers in factories who are not only working off their own mental conflicts on others to the detriment of the psychological health of the community but are psychologically incapable of delegating authority and making industry more democratic.[3]

One cannot, then, overstate the importance of good leadership and its effects on outcomes. Furthermore, leadership has a profound effect on people too, perhaps less obviously in the sense that employees are always asking, overtly or covertly, to be led. They want leadership because leadership removes ambiguity for them as well as potentially absolving them from responsibility: 'Follow the leader' because it is too much to be asked to perform one's tasks, one's role, and at the same time to work out where we are going and how we are going to get there. This is not to denigrate people's capacity for leadership or their ability to surprise when placed in positions of leadership, but it reflects what happens on the ground. Without stretching the analogy too far, and, as we said before, we want to be like bees in a hive whose work makes honey, but for bees to be productive there needs to be a queen, a leader; and without the leader there can be no 'organisation', as the removal of the queen demonstrates.

ACTIVITY 2

If leadership is so important, it is a good idea to reflect on what it is. Write down your definition of leadership. What is it? What does it do? What properties are essential for it to be healthy and effective? What effects do you note or wish for from good leadership?

How do you detect poor or weak or bad leadership? What qualities signify its presence? How do you think we can improve leadership in organisations? What one thing, if it could be done, would improve the quality of leadership the most?

According to Dwight Eisenhower, 'Leadership is the ability to get a man[4] to do what you want him to do, when you want it done, in a way you want it done, because he wants to do it.' Easy? During the twentieth century four broad theories underpinning views on leadership developed. They all teach us something; they all contain some truths; but they also indicate the general confusion around the topic, and its lack of clarity. What is light? As Dr Johnson observed, 'We all know what it is, but it is difficult to *say* what it is.' In short, we all 'sort of' recognise it when we see it in action, but saying what it is can be tricky. What we must avoid, since this book is practical, is becoming too academic about it; we need practical models that work in the real world and make a difference. Perfection can often be the enemy of progress.

With that in mind, the four main theories of leadership are: Trait, Behavioural, Contingency, and Attributional. In brief, Trait theories attempt to identify the characteristics of leaders: is there a common 'set'? Its corollary is that people are born leaders. Another corollary tends to be the search for 'strong' leaders – that is, those who have the 'set'. But 'strong' frequently becomes synonymous, certainly post-war, with authoritarian traits. One of the serious problems with Trait theory is the failure to find an agreed 'set' of traits. But four personality traits that are commonly thought to be associated with leadership are: dominance, responsibility, achievement, and self-assurance. However, are they, at all times and in all situations?

Behavioural theories, on the other hand, given that a set of traits cannot be certainly established, focus on preferable leadership actions. What do good leaders do? Such behaviours, it is argued, since not innate, could be developed by training. Two dimensions of this are in seeing leadership as being about task-orientation (employees getting the job done, having clear responsibilities, meeting deadlines, and so on) and people-orientation (relationship aspects of their work – trust, mutual respect and regard, team-building, and so on). That said, Behavioural theories run into the same problems as Trait – identifying a common set of behaviours that are universally applicable was and is found difficult.

Despite their considerable insights, many found both theories inadequate. Contingency theory attempted to identify situational variables that would influence outcomes. The key aspect of this work is to consider how one leadership approach, whilst being relevant and successful in one situation, becomes invalid in another. In other words – and as the description 'situational' suggests – leadership all depends on finding the appropriate style to match the actual condition that is being encountered.[5] The four most important variables that Contingency likes to consider as making a difference to leadership outcomes are: degree of structure in the task; the quality of relationships between the leader and employees; the leader's position power;[6] and environment. But there are many more,[7] and this list of ever-increasing variables means that Contingency theories ultimately become complex and divorced from 'common sense'. This makes them difficult to apply in practical situations.[8] That said, they have produced interesting insights into how leadership can be more effective, and furthermore it does seem common sense that different situations do require different leadership styles.

Finally, Attributional theory addresses the difficulties of situational analysis by suggesting that leadership is what people characterise leaders as having. This, then, is a perceptual view of leadership; its interpretation hinges on what people perceive as 'real'. So, for example, people characterise effective leaders as being consistent. The immediate advantage of this approach is its common sense; it strikes a chord precisely because it registers how people think about leaders. In this way it almost takes us full circle to Trait theories, because they seem self-evident too. Trait predicates people as having the qualities; Attributional theory predicates that people perceive leaders as having particular qualities. For example, leaders are perceived as having charisma, intelligence, strong personalities, verbal skills, aggressiveness, industriousness, and so on.[9]

So with all this behind us, where do we go from here? W.E. Deming observed that 'All theories are false, but some are useful.' My starting point is to understand what skills leaders generically *have* to have, and which can be built on – so avoiding the dead-end of believing that leaders can only be born, not made – and at the same time to try to address the inherent ambiguity and uncertainty in leadership, and leaders themselves. In other words, we need a model that on the one hand can build on what can certainly be built on, but at the same time leaves some space for the messy, almost anarchic and emotional 'people bit'.

To this end, then, Motivational Maps have developed what they call their '4+1' model of leadership. It would seem that four plus one equals five; but that's the point of the equation: that four apples plus one orange does not make five apples! There are four key skills that can be built on, that we can identify and do something about. But there is a 'fifth' or +1 point that is qualitatively different from the skill sets. It is far more important in real terms than the other four skills, as massively important as those skills are, and yet it is the least – certainly in my experience – considered and valued of all the issues concerning leadership. Indeed, if it is considered at all, it is usually as an afterthought or an optional extra. Yet it is the key, because it goes into the invisible, into the ambiguous; in fact, it goes into the soul of human beings.

But first, what are these four core skills?

ACTIVITY 3

What do you think are the four most important skills that a leader should have in discharging their duties?

There are two main aspects of leadership that any leader has to be thoroughly conversant with. First, leaders must be able to work ON the organisation (or ON the business).[10] What does that mean? In essence this reduces to two major skills: the Thinking about the organisation and the Doing for the organisation. Leaders need to be able to think and to do, but in very specific ways. The Thinking is about the vision and strategy for the organisation and the Doing is about the implementation of the processes, systems, and structures that enable the strategy to be delivered. And when we consider these two aspects of leadership most of us will surely be aware of occasions when these two skills are not in balance: namely, the visionary and strategic leader who has all the ideas but no follow-through; and equally as badly the technocrat who has every process and system down to a tee, but the organisation lacks vision and heart.

Figures 8.1 and 8.2 give more details concerning what specific skills are involved under the wide umbrellas of Thinking and Doing. The skills are not exhaustive, but should give a clear idea of what is important and what is in mind here.

Secondly, the leader has to work IN the organisation (or business). This working IN is not about the systems, as in the Doing; it is about recruiting, creating, and sustaining the winning teams. Such teams seriously leverage human productivity. As we said in Chapter 6: Together Each Achieves More. But the final part of working IN drills down to the individual: the leader must not only build the strong,

LEADERSHIP "THINKING" ABOUT THE ORGANIZATION

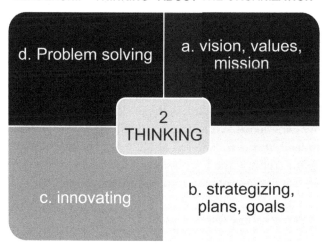

Figure 8.1   4+1 motivational leadership Thinking

LEADERSHIP "DOING" THE ORGANIZATION

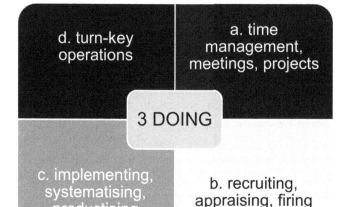

Figure 8.2   4+1 motivational leadership Doing

ACTIVITY 4

Go through the list of Thinking and Doing skills in Figures 8.1 and 8.2 and create a checklist of those you think essential. Add any that you think may be missing. Now rate yourself, or a leader you have in mind, out of 10 for each of the skills (10 being highly rated and 1 being poorly rated). The lowest scores will be the Achilles heel of your or that person's leadership performance. How important is that skill and how fatal is it if it is weak or absent?

winning teams; they must also motivate every individual in the organisation, for it is the motivation that will provide the biggest impact on performance.[11]

As with Figures 8.1 and 8.2 for Thinking and Doing, so Figures 8.3 and 8.4 indicate some further aspects of what is involved in building teams and motivating employees. The terminology here will be more familiar as it has been the subject of earlier chapters, and indeed of this whole book. For we now see that leadership is intimately connected with the skills of developing people,

LEADERSHIP AND BUILDING THE TEAMS

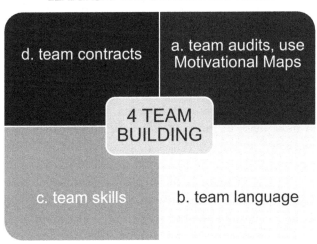

Figure 8.3   4+1 motivational leadership Team Building

LEADERSHIP AND MOTIVATING EMPLOYEES

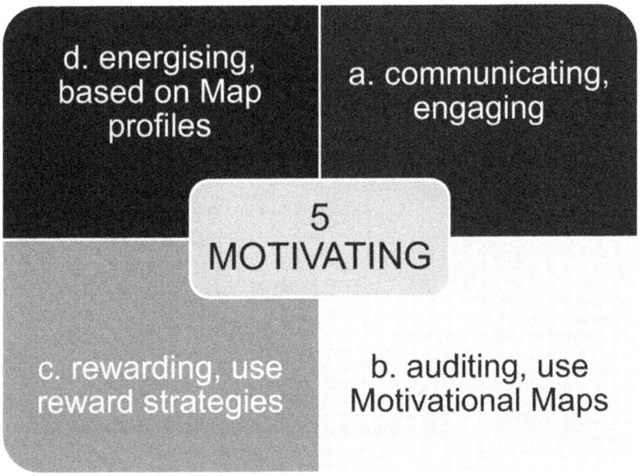

Figure 8.4   4+1 motivational leadership Motivating

whether that be through teams or individually through motivation. I will come back to this point again shortly, but before I do there is still one missing aspect of this 4+1 Motivational Leadership Model.

Generically, then, the leader must work ON the organisation (strategy and delivery systems) and work IN the organisation (teams and individual motivations) too. These are the big four skills we mentioned earlier; but, as I said before, whilst these are mission critical, they are yet still not enough. There is something vital missing from this leadership picture; something that is not a skill, something that is not easily classifiable but without which leadership is doomed in the long run. Keep in mind, the 'long run' is where all value organisations (and businesses) need and want to be.

The full 4+1 Motivational Leadership Model looks like Figure 8.5. Four core skills are underpinned by the Self and the necessity for self-development – or, personal development if you will. Sometimes, unfortunately, you encounter teachers who have been in the profession for 20 years and allegedly have 20 years' experience; but what that can mean in reality is that they have one year's experience which they have been repeating over and over in the same way for 20 years! They use the same lesson notes to deliver the same lessons. And you meet this frequently in leadership: people who 10, 20, or even 30 years ago received some training and development on management or leadership, got promoted, went up the ladder but have never had any development, formal or informal, since. What they are doing increasingly,

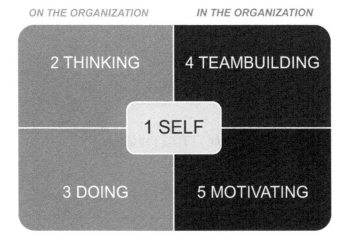

Figure 8.5   4+1 Motivational Leadership Model

in fact, is attempting to solve today's organisational and business problems with yesterday's understanding, skill set and self-identity. And that is why we often see leaders who once were successful but who now head up teams or organisations where their contributions are progressively more and more insubstantial and irrelevant.[12]

Thus the leader must be committed to their own personal development, their own growth, and their own learning if they are to be effective. Without that commitment and action, leadership is running on empty – and it soon shows. Figure 8.6 gives some of the components of what personal or self-development might look like.

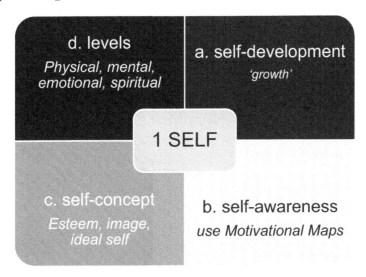

Figure 8.6   4+1 motivational leadership and the Self

Perhaps the single most important thing of all to stress in the model is self-awareness and the need to constantly expand it, for without self-awareness no growth is possible. One of the curious paradoxes of true and deep learning, and of the real experts who truly have become 'gurus' in their field, is their almost universal testimony to the fact that the greater the expertise they have, the greater their awareness is of all that they don't know. Their self-awareness of what they know contrasts ever more vividly with the scale of what they don't know, and this itself has a personal growth effect in that it seems to engender humility and a real willingness and desire (motivation) to learn even more. Contrast this with the 'know-it-all', the person with a tiny bit of knowledge in a tiny field, who remains stuck in the rut of their extremely limited competence.

So Figure 8.7 and others mention the Motivational Maps in connection with this process since the book is about motivation; but clearly self-awareness is a much wider topic than merely knowing one's own motivators. Any diagnostic tool can potentially assist in this process, as will feedback from others.

ACTIVITY 5

How important is self-awareness to you? Would you describe yourself as 'self-aware'? If yes, what proof do you have that that is so? If not, then why not? What has prevented you from being self-aware? What could you do to increase your self-awareness? Do you have a process for developing self-awareness? What tools might help you increase your self-awareness?

Five cost-effective ways to improve your self-awareness are:

1.   acquiring quality feedback

2.   using diagnostic profiling tools

3.   starting a journal

4.   challenging yourself to leave your 'comfort zone'

5.   and, finally, imagining.[13]

ACTIVITY 6

Do not attempt to become more self-aware by undertaking all five ways simultaneously. Instead, choose one way that appeals to you and make a plan to work it for at least six months, and to track your progress.

1.   Where and who will you get good-quality feedback from? Consider the feedback that might help you in the following areas: your qualities, your performance/capabilities, and your situation. List the people you know, like, and trust – who can help? When and how will you ask them? What organisations can help you? How can you access them and their expertise? From a strictly leadership point of view, acquiring a coach or mentor can turbo-charge your performance precisely because of the quality of feedback that they can provide.

2.   What diagnostic profiles will you complete? Motivational Maps is one tool; what about personality tests or psychometric assessments? Consider strengths and weakness inventories, or team or learning styles diagnostics like Belbin and Kolb. What will you do with them when they

ACTIVITY 6 (cont.)

are done? One thing might be to ask somebody who knows you well to comment on the accuracy of the profiles(s). Another key task is to compare the type of person you are with the type of work you do – is there a fit?

3. Review your own life in detail: what you have done speaks volumes about the real 'you', not the imaginary 'you' or the false 'you' that you have inadvertently constructed over time in your own mind. When will you start your own journal? Log at least three achievements per day. Review your week and month regularly, spot patterns. What have you achieved over the last three days specifically? Remember, this is a key issue in building self-esteem; it builds a portfolio of evidence that becomes believable even to the subconscious mind – yours.

4. Challenge yourself to leave your comfort zone. What activity will you undertake? Usually new learning is necessary to do something never done before. What would make you proud if you did it? What did you want to do as a child or young person, but never did? What would give you a real stretch? Remember, if all this seems difficult, that children do this all the time: they sing in public for the first time; they undertake complex work; they go on some adventure trek – and as a result they grow at a tremendous rate. They drive themselves to their limits. One word of caution: going out of the comfort zone is not to be confused with doing bizarre and dangerous things just because they are there, or because others do them.

5. Imagining ... or daydreaming and asking 'what if?' When will you visualise? How? And under what conditions? Stay relaxed. Make notes ... visualise yourself with knowledge, skills, talents that appeal to you. By focusing your mind on what you want, or even on finding what you want, a powerful force is unleashed. The power of the imagination is virtually unlimited; everything that is came into existence via the imagination: it was seen in the mind's eye before it was 'created' literally or physically. Thus the more time spent imagining ideal 'realities', the more likely it is that that reality will come to pass. It is important that when using visualisation and imaging techniques that you stay in a relaxed state of mind.

These five techniques will certainly boost self-awareness and understanding of one's strengths and weaknesses; they are, therefore, indispensable (in their selective way) to the whole idea of developing effective leadership. We have covered the four skills, which also need developing, as well as the essential personal development aspect of leadership, albeit briefly, and hopefully in a way that suggests what further needs to be done. But there is another point to be made, since this is a book about motivation.

If we grant the fact that the model is useful and, if not perfect, at least a big step forward in terms of addressing the issue of how we develop leaders, then we are faced with a startling fact which is scarcely noticed in the literature about leadership. Namely, just how much of leadership is really about motivation. Indeed, if we look at the 4+1 model element by element what do we see?

We see that working IN the business is almost wholly about motivation: the creation of teams is more than just sticking people together who have the 'right' skill and knowledge set, as Chapter 6 on teams has made clear. Self-evidently, the need for the leader to motivate their team, and more widely their organisation, is paramount if performance is to be optimised. But then we move to working ON the business. Here we note that the vision and strategy element is not motivationally driven, but the DOING is where it concerns key implementation activities and systems such as recruitment and performance appraisals. Finally, when we consider the heart of it all – the '+1', the personal or self-development – we see that developing self-awareness is something the Motivational Maps can make a major contribution to; and further, the strengthening of the self-esteem is linked to beliefs, the very thing in Chapter 2 that underpins motivation. In short, there is a big overlap.

If we then consider all this together it might successfully be argued that a full 50% of leadership comes down to motivation: the leader being motivated, motivating others, ensuring new recruits are motivated, sustaining motivation, motivating teams, and so on. Thus, contrary to what we expect or what we typically experience, motivation is at the core of leadership; there is scarcely a more important area for the leader to master. But, as we discussed in Chapter 1, its ambiguity is why it gets less attention and more avoidance than it should. The creation of Motivational Maps with its language and metrics is a step forward in reversing this trend.

And reversing this trend is critical if another trend is also going to be reversed: a recent study by Gallup found that only 13% of employees worldwide are engaged at work.[14] Engagement is the new big issue that has arisen over the last 15 years or so; it is new, but it is also familiar. It has arisen for two primary reasons: firstly, the shift from Taylorism to the psychology of business and the psychology of the employees in it. This is most obviously seen in the simple change of title: Personnel departments have become Human Resources (HR) departments. In other words, people are 'human' assets, and that is more than just a unit of production. A new approach is needed then. Secondly, there has been in the last 20 years a real increase of scientific interest in what Maslow began some 50 or so years ago: namely, the work of Martin Seligman and others in positive psychological states.[15] The importance of this is in realising that so much emphasis before had been on describing negative states, which somehow became normative – which is like focusing on the causes of misery and imagining thereby one could be happy.

ACTIVITY 7

What does engagement mean to and for you? What do you observe about engagement in your workplace and in other workplaces? For example, everybody experiences other people's level of engagement when we employ a service from them: when we enter shops, bars and restaurants; when we go to swimming pools, cinemas, social clubs; when we are visited by utility and maintenance workers and inspectors; when we connect on the landline or mobile to customer service centres. In these situations we cannot help but notice whether the employees are engaged or not. What do you find? What difference might being fully engaged as an employee make to you as a customer? What difference might it make to your organisation if you or other employees were more fully engaged? How do you think employees might be more engaged?

There is no one model of what employee engagement is or how it works; a cursory look at the American versus the British experience shows wide variations. But the role of motivation in all this can hardly be overstated. In my experience I would describe motivation as comprising some 70% of the engagement mix. According to Schaufeli the best model explaining the underlying psychological mechanisms of employee engagement is the Job Demands Resources model, and this constantly refers to the growing weight of evidence for the 'dynamic nature of the motivational process … as far as job performance is concerned'.[16] Chris Burton put it this way:

> The relationship between engagement and motivation is a two way street; improve one and you also improve the other. So the key to understanding how to benefit from improved levels of engagement is firstly to understand what motivates us – why do we really do the things we do … ? To understand what really motivates us we need to strip away all the factors which might merely influence us; in other words, we need to identify what lies at the very heart of our motivation to do something.[17]

What is important, then, is not to go further into describing engagement models, but to realise that if we want engagement in our organisations, then we cannot escape the imperative for addressing motivation. In more simple terms, engagement can be seen as a behaviour which is sustained and directed by an internal energy,[18] an energy that is best described as motivation.[19] Clearly, behaviours are not all fuelled by motivation; it's easy enough to have employees behaving as they ought to behave, but without being engaged at all. The challenge is to get them behaving in a way that is commensurate with organisational objectives not because it is their job or role, but because they want to. Remember that part of the Eisenhower definition of leadership which says 'because he wants to do it'. When someone wants to do it, then they are motivated.

What would now be useful, then, is to consider not only the fact that we can target individuals, teams, and whole organisations in a precise way to stimulate their specific motivators and motivational profile, but also to realise that the primary 'drivers' for engagement have also got a motivational dimension. Research by Towers Perrin identified 10 key drivers of employee engagement, shown in Figure 8.7 in order of importance.[20]

ACTIVITY 8

What do you think are the top 10 activities or conditions or drivers that would promote employee engagement? How likely is management to implement such drivers where you work or where you observe work? What prevents management from engaging in employee engagement? What might motivate them to do so?

1	Senior management sincerely interested in employee well-being
2	Improved my skills and capabilities over the last year
3	Organisation's reputation for social responsibility
4	Input into decision making in my department
5	Organisation quickly resolves customer concerns
6	Set high personal standards
7	Have excellent career advancement opportunities
8	Enjoy challenging work assignments that broaden skills
9	Good relationship with supervisor
10	Organisation encourages innovative thinking

Figure 8.7   Top 10 drivers of employee engagement

But when we think of each of these drivers in turn, we realise that management – people – must deliver them, indeed, must want to deliver them if there is to be any likelihood that they will happen. But what motivators will drive them to happen? And of course, given that all 10 drivers are different, then it will come as no surprise that the combination of motivators that is likely to want to deliver the engagement 'package' is likely to be unique for each combination.

Let's take the number one driver of employee engagement: namely, that senior management is sincerely interested in employee well-being. If we imagine that we have a management team who are dominantly motivated by the Builder, or money, motivator, then are they likely to be 'sincerely interested'? Hardly, except as a by-product of the calculation that if we feign interest employees might be more engaged; but then that's hardly 'sincere' is it? And employees have a nose for this sort of phoniness. But it's not just the Builder. What if Spirit is the dominant motivator, or we have a classic sales combination of Spirit and Builder together in the management team? Managers looking for their own autonomy are usually not those 'sincerely interested' in employee well-being.

ACTIVITY 9

So do the sums for yourself. What are the best three motivators that would help drive employee engagement from a management team? I'll help by suggesting the answers to the top driver. This, paradoxically (but unsurprisingly for those who have studied this book carefully), is likely to be the Relationship motivators: Friend, Defender, and Star in that order of importance. Friend, I hope, self-evidently; Defender because communication would be in triplicate and guaranteed; and Star because giving recognition would go a long way. This is not to say having another motivational profile means the drivers cannot be delivered, but it makes it harder and less likely. Go through, then, the remaining nine drivers and ask yourself what you think are the top three motivators that would enable this most successfully to occur.

This chapter has focused on leadership and engagement, and in one true sense only scratched the surface; but if there is one key thing that it has sought to establish, it is this: that motivation is at the heart and soul of both leadership and engagement, and all attempts to address and improve these two issues without reference to motivation, the motivation of employees first and leaders second, are doomed to fall short.

1	Senior management sincerely interested in employee well-being	Relationship motivators	
2	Ability to improve skills and capabilities	Achievement motivators	
3	Organisation's reputation for social responsibility	Relationship motivators	
4	Employees inputs into decision making	Mixed motivators	
5	Quick resolution of customer concerns	Mixed motivators	
6	Setting of high personal standards	Mixed motivators	
7	Excellent career advancement opportunities	Mixed motivators	
8	Challenging work assignments that broaden skills	Mixed motivators	
9	Good relationships with supervisors	Mixed motivators	
10	Organisation encourages innovative thinking	Mixed motivators	

Figure 8.8   Motivational drivers for employee engagement[21]

Summary

1.   Leadership is the number one factor in organisational success; employees need leadership, want good leadership, because they want to be led so that they can be productive.

2.   We all recognise good and bad leadership when we see it, but it is difficult to define leadership.

3.   There are four main theories of leadership – Trait, Behavioural, Contingency, and Attributional – and all have useful things to teach us, although none of them may be entirely accurate.

4.   We need a model that is simple, practical, and useful, and which enables us to improve leadership whilst at the same time recognising

its innate ambiguity. The 4+1 Motivational Leadership Model aims to do just that.

5.   There are four key skills of leadership: two for working ON the organisation (thinking and doing); and two that work IN the organisation (team building and motivating).

6.   However, the heart of leadership is about personal growth and development, without which the leader is trying to solve today's problems with yesterday's knowledge, skills, and self.

7.   There is a deficit of employee engagement in the workplace worldwide, and leadership needs to address this issue.

8.   Despite different models of what engagement is, all employee engagement involves of necessity addressing the motivations of employees and of leaders too.

9.   The 10 top 'drivers' of employee engagement are themselves driven by specific motivational profiles.

Notes

[1]   'Senior leadership is regarded as the most critical driver of sustainability within a business and nearly half of businesses (44%) believe engagement with business leaders will be the most important factor in successfully implementing a sustainability strategy over the next three years.' – Economist Intelligence Unit (EIU) and Coca-Cola Enterprises, *Sustainability Insights: Learning from Business Leaders*, 2013; also, 'Deloitte found that companies viewed as having particularly strong leadership could enjoy a stock market valuation premium of more than 15 per cent. Those seen as having ineffective leadership suffered discounts of up to 20 per cent' – David Wighton, Investors agree that quality of leadership is crucial for high performance, *The Times*, 12 June 2012.

[2]   Norman F. Dixon, *On the Psychology of Military Incompetence*, London: Futura, 1982.

[3]   J.A.C. Brown, *The Social Psychology of Industry*, Harmondsworth: Penguin, 1958, p. 294.

[4]   Or woman of course.

[5]   See Michael Barber (ex-head of the UK Government's Effectiveness Unit) on leadership, *The Learning Game: Arguments for an Education Revolution*, London: Gollancz, 1996 (pp. 119, 131, 237–8): 'there is a need to study at a more sophisticated level the characteristics of successful leadership. We all know it is a decisive factor, but what are its essential elements? Do they differ according to context? Does the leader of a school in the process of being "turned around" need different skills and qualities from the leader of an already successful school?' Notice the hesitancy in the question, 'Do they differ according to context?' This commendable caution suggests that the question isn't rhetorical, and that he doesn't know the answer. This indicates the level of complexity that leadership involves. We do well to remember this when presented with 'answers'.

[6]   Position power – as distinct from personal/charismatic or technical power – is the degree to which the 'boss' has the power to hire, fire, discipline, promote, and control salaries.

[7]   For example, staff role clarity, group norms, information availability, staff acceptance of leader's decisions, staff maturity, etc.

[8]   The exception to this stricture seems to be John Adair's action-centred model of leadership. Adair posited that success in leadership depended on effectiveness in three crucial areas: task needs, group needs, and individual needs.

[9]   Mike Hudson, *Managing Without Profit* (London: Penguin, 1995), cites research in America with over 2,500 managers who ranked the four most important qualities of leadership (in order of importance) as: honesty – keeps agreements, tells the truth, is trustworthy; competence – good track record, challenges, enables, encourages; forward-looking attitude – sense of direction, sense of destination; capacity to inspire – communicates vision, gives people a sense of worth.

[10] Michael Gerber, in his book *The E-Myth* (Cambridge, MA: Ballinger, 1986), is primarily credited for making this distinction for entrepreneurs working ON their businesses as opposed to working IN them.

[11] It might be argued that motivating people is a leader's skill that is not only inwardly focused on staff, but outwardly focused on suppliers, customers, and the wider audience of the world's opinion too. We might call this sales, PR, or even negotiation. All require positive energy.

[12] David Clutterbuck expressed it this way: 'People who stop learning become less and less useful.'

[13] I am indebted to Dave Francis' *Managing Your Own Career* (London, Fontana, 1985) for these ideas.

[14] Gallup's 142-country study on the State of the Global Workplace, 2012. It also found the majority of employees worldwide – 63% – are 'not engaged', meaning they lack motivation and are less likely to invest discretionary effort in organisational goals or outcomes; also that 24% are 'actively disengaged', indicating they are unhappy and unproductive at work and liable to spread negativity to co-workers. Approximately, this means about 900 million employees are not engaged and 340 million are actively disengaged workers around the world.

[15] Martin Seligman, *Learned Optimism*, New York: Knopf, 1991; also, Mihaly Csíkszentmihalyi, *Flow: The Psychology of Happiness*, New York: Harper and Row, 1990.

[16] Wilmar B. Schaufeli, What is engagement?, in C. Truss, K. Alfes, R. Delbridge, A. Shantz, and E. Soane (eds), *Employee Engagement in Theory and Practice*, Abingdon: Routledge, 2013, pp. 26, 28 – 'Essentially, the Job Demands-Resources model assumes that work engagement results from the inherently motivating nature of resources, whereby two types of resources are distinguished: (1) job resources, which are defined as those aspects of the job that are functional in achieving work goals, reduce job demands, or stimulate personal growth and development (e.g., performance feedback, job control, and social support from colleagues); (2) personal resources, which are defined as aspects of the self that are associated with resiliency and that refer to the ability to control and impact one's environment successfully (e.g., self-efficacy, optimism and emotional stability).'

[17] Chris Burton, White Paper, A study into Motivation: Why we *really* do the things we do ... (2012/13), http://www.t-three.com/worklife-motivation/downloads/MotivationWhitePaper.pdf.

[18] David Bowles and Cary Cooper, *The High Engagement Work Culture*, Basingstoke: Palgrave Macmillan, 2012.

[19] As opposed, for example, to morale, or attitude, or commitment, or some other synonymous term.

[20] *Employee Engagement: A Towers Perrin Study*, 2009.

[21] For a comprehensive breakdown of what each motivator the motivational logos refer to see Figure R.1 in the Resources section.

Chapter 9

Motivation in Practice: Two Case Studies

What is important in all these ideas about motivation, performance, teams, leadership, and engagement (to mention some of the important concepts we have explored in this book) is that we can action them in the real world, and that they make a positive difference. The final chapter, then, is an extended meditation on two case studies in which Motivational Maps has been introduced to bridge that gap from where the organisation is to where it wants to be. It should come as no surprise that in order to bridge the gap all organisations have to do it via people; it is the only way. Each organisation is a vehicle, if you like, which exists to make an important journey, to achieve some undertaking, to provide some contribution that the world wants and values and will pay for. Thus it is that, as we said before, all vehicles need fuel, and that fuel is motivation; there is simply no escaping it. If you want to drive anywhere, then top your tank with motivation so that you don't run out and find yourself on empty before you arrive.

I would like to provide some notes on the two studies, which are quite extended, so that the reader can get a real feel for what has happened and why, and furthermore, so that they can see – warts and all – what the issues are. Hopefully from this they will be able to identify its relevance to their own organisation, their own teams; indeed their own leadership and change issues.

The first comment I would like to make about the case studies and about Mapping Motivation more generally is that this process is always about, and highly geared towards, change management. When we think of change management in an organisational sense, then we have a pretty clear idea of what is entailed in this; but change management also affects teams and individuals. We are all changing all the time; sometimes in small, barely noticeable steps, but other times in huge, perceptible strides. And the point that has been made many times in this book is that energy is underpinning all change; energy, or motivation, is enabling all change to occur. If that is the case, how can ignoring motivation be a sensible strategy for an organisation, team, or individual to adopt?

When we review the first case study, which was initially a year-long programme with Ordnance Survey, we notice some of the key words and phrases that change is really all about: words like communication, buzz, shared language, understanding, conversations, dialogue, conflict, teams, leadership development, and ownership. These are important words that denote the conditions under which significant and substantial change is possible. This is true of Ordnance Survey, given its status and ethos, and true too of our second case study, the John Lewis Partnership, which is an organisation not publicly owned (that is, through shares), but partner-owned – a co-operative. Effective communication in both organisations must assume a paramount level of priority; and this is doubly so because, note, such organisations place a premium on values and ethics, not just for their customers/clients but also for their suppliers and employees. Given this, it should come as no surprise then that it is precisely these types of organisation that experience the 'longevity' that we talked about in Chapter 1.[1]

With this in mind, Jayne Beresford, Ordnance Survey Organisational Development Consultant, outlines what happened and why. Here is her account.

Motivational Maps at Ordnance Survey

Ordnance Survey (OS) started to use Motivational Maps in May 2014.

WHO ARE WE?

OS is Britain's mapping agency. We make the most up-to-date and accurate maps of the country. But we're also a digital business, and we use our content to help governments, companies and individuals become more effective both here and around the world.

OS data helps emergency services to respond faster, keeps transport flowing, enables utilities companies to locate their assets, helps mortgage lenders and insurers to assess risks, claims and more.

At OS we employ around 1,200 employees and have a proud heritage of investing in our people. As a result we have been able to constantly grow and change in response to our ever changing market demands. Around 1,000 of our employees are based at a head office building in Southampton and a number of field surveying and sales roles are remotely based in order to cover the whole of Britain.

WHY MOTIVATIONAL MAPS?

We started to use Motivational Maps in 2014 in our Commercial business group (around 150 people) and our Marketing and Communications business group (around 40 people). We had just appointed new directors to lead each of these groups. They needed to work closely together and needed their people to have the right levels of skills, knowledge, and motivation to achieve the commercial aspirations of the organisation. Andrew Loveless, the Commercial Director, was particularly keen to use the Motivational Map tool to enhance the motivation and therefore performance of his directorate. He describes the challenge he faced and his reasoning behind Motivational Maps:

> *We needed to understand what was driving and motivating our sales force. It was important to get to the very core level of what drove the team. We had a very ambitious growth agenda and needed a common framework to have an open dialogue around the motivators we had in the business. We wanted to do something purposefully different. I'd seen the Motivational Maps work well in a previous context and was keen to leverage that output again.*

Figure 9.1   Andrew Loveless, Commercial Director, Ordnance Survey

The challenge that Katie Powell, Marketing and Communications Director, faced was around forming an entirely new directorate within the organisation and creating a shared focus:

> *We were forming a totally new function of Marketing and Communications. Marketing itself had previously had six different reporting lines within the business and no focal point. We had to root out and pull together people to understand their common purpose and bring them together as a team. As we were working predominantly with what we had we were asking many people to step up and giving them a stretch so we had to understand the make-up of the team. We had a good idea of skills but not so much of what drove them and that was essential.*

Figure 9.2   Katie Powell, Marketing and Communications Director, Ordnance Survey

WHAT DID WE DO?

We worked with James Sale to run a 'train the trainer' model across these business groups, effectively training up the two senior management teams in order that they could then train their own managers and people around the meaning and use of the Motivational Maps. The programme played out as follows:

Month 1	James delivered a session to introduce the concept of Motivational Maps to the Commercial and Marketing and Communications senior management teams (13 people in total).
	All attending these sessions then received links to complete their own Motivational Maps questionnaires.
Month 2	James delivered 'day 1' training to both senior management teams to enable them to understand their own Motivational Maps and make individual action plans around enhancing their own motivation levels.
	All senior managers introduced the concept of Motivational Maps to their own teams; shared what they had found useful; and highlighted that they would be guiding their teams through their own results when they had completed their own questionnaires.
	All individuals across the two business groups were invited to complete their own questionnaires.
	Upon completion the questionnaires were sent to each individual automatically so that they could read about and understand their own levels of motivation.
Month 3	James delivered 'day 2' training to both senior management teams to enable them to understand the motivators of their own teams and create action plans for how they were going to work with and enhance these.
	Each senior manager then delivered a team session to their own team to explain Motivational Maps in more depth, share results, and support individuals in their teams to come up with their own Motivational Maps action plans.
	Each senior manager also delivered a separate session to their own management team to enable them to understand their team Motivational Maps, where key areas of action were, and to form team action plans.
Month 4 onwards	All managers and individuals were encouraged to continue to use Motivational Maps to enable meaningful conversations in 1:1s.
	All individuals were given an open invite to complete the Motivational Maps at any point they needed to (e.g. significant changes in personal circumstances).
Month 7	All individuals (including senior managers and directors) across the two business groups were invited to complete the Motivational Maps questionnaires again in order to see how motivational profiles had changed.
Month 8	James delivered masterclasses to all managers across the two business groups, looking at a combination of their own and their team motivation results, in order to review what actions had worked in the last round and plan next motivational action steps.

HOW DID PEOPLE REACT TO THE MOTIVATIONAL MAPS?

At an individual level most people found the Motivational Map questionnaire easy to complete and found the Motivational Map reports to be quite self-explanatory:

> *They were quick to complete, quicker than a lot of questionnaires.*

> *The reports were easy to understand. Good colour coding, easy to read bar charts of results.*

> *I was able to understand my profile quickly so could then move on to investing my energy in what to do to improve my motivation.*

While some were quite sceptical of its simplicity initially, a lot of people commented that the outputs were personally insightful for them:

> *I tutted and groaned all through the seemingly 'daft' questions ... and then it came up with something uncannily spot on! Very clever.*

WHAT WAS THE IMPACT OF THE MAPS?

The biggest impact from the initial round of Motivational Map questionnaires across the two directorates was the buzz they created. Many people talked about their motivation preferences and shared their results with colleagues, and this created a shared language and sense of wider team. In order to support and grow this buzz, the senior management teams had set the tone by publically sharing their own Motivational Maps results and how they had found them useful.

Managers at all levels across these business groups picked out that the key positive with Motivational Maps was the conversations that they enabled with their people. Miranda Sharp, Head of Commercial Markets within the Commercial Directorate, comments:

> *They were a useful conversation starter. They enabled meaningful conversations between managers and individuals and gave us a shared language to use across the team.*

The Maps also seemed to create a shared agenda between managers and their people due to the visibility of motivation results to both. They allowed conversations at a meaningful and non-threatening level as they could start around the context of motivation and work from there rather than starting around performance.

Andrew Loveless, Commercial Director, reports on the power of the Motivational Maps with his own direct reports:

> *The Maps enabled laser precision, actionable insights, nothing is genericised. In working to empower my own leadership team there was intense moments of self-realisation and powerful conversations as a result.*

The Motivational Maps results also appeared to enable more macro insights across the team. Katie Powell, Marketing and Communications Director:

> It was interesting to see how individuals mapped. It gave managers a different lens to see their team through and enabled managers to see where conflicts may be occurring across the teams.

WHAT CHANGES IN MOTIVATION DID WE FIND?

At the time of writing we have data from an initial set of Motivational Maps questionnaires and from the follow-up set around six months later. Looking at the changes in motivation across this time frame at a purely numerical level, the picture has been very varied across individuals. The biggest increase in motivation was 38% and the biggest decrease was -44%. For about half of each group motivation went up over the six months and for the other half motivation went down. As a result of this variation in both directions the average motivation level across the whole of the two directorates remained roughly stable over the six months, at just under 70% motivated for both business groups at both time points.

The individual with the biggest increase in motivation over the six months (an increase of 38%) worked within the Public Sector team in the Commercial business group. This whole team saw stability in a high level of motivation at a team level (from 69% to 70%). The Director of this team, John Kimmance, comments on the usefulness of the Maps both personally and as the lead of a team of managers with their own teams to manage:

> Knowing my motivators helped me to think about the role and how to do more of what motivates me in it. For example, the recognition of having Spirit in my profile made me look at where I could take more autonomy in my role. It also helped in conversations on the drive to manage my own ship without any micro-management from above … having applied the learning to yourself you could then apply it to your team … one of my managers has a high Defender in his profile and we are in an environment where we have to grow and change constantly. The awareness of the maps has enabled a light-hearted level of conversation around this, and also means that I take a bit more time to bring him up to speed on our constant changes to help him become comfortable with them.

In the case of the individual within this team whose motivation had improved by 38%, he and his manager worked through the Motivational Maps results together in an open and structured way, looking at his top motivators, how well they were being met, and whether they were a good fit for the role he had moved into. They used these to plan the individual's goals and developments and actions to build on current motivators. They also used the lowest motivators as a check to see if anything in the individual's development plan was conflicting. This individual describes his story in depth below and explains how a combination of factors, many purposely driven by the Motivational Maps, enabled his motivation to improve so significantly:

> I used to work in a different part of the business but had grown a little stale and was meeting a brick wall in trying to progress. I took the decision to move out of this environment into the commercial role. At the time of completing my first questionnaire I had just accepted the role but hadn't started it. My top three motivators at that time were Builder, Spirit, and Creator and my motivation level was 54%. With Builder as my highest motivator the move to the Commercial part of the business seemed to fit me really well, and completing the Map drove home that awareness. My manager and I worked together with the Motivational Maps and were able to use them to build on the good relationship we had. My manager was better able to understand me and to fit his management style to my needs. For example, in order to meet the Spirit motivator, my manager now gives me the whole problem in a project to develop and manage. He keeps in touch and is there if I need him, but he allows me to own the whole piece so I feel it is mine and I have that independence. We were able to fit my work goals better to my needs as well. It has also given me insights into how to motivate myself more. For the Builder motivator I started to work well to challenge myself and reward myself for achieving my goals. I was also better able to tell my line manager how I needed to be managed to get the best out of me. My motivation is now at 92% and, interestingly, my top three are now the blues [Growth motivators], whereas the middle three are the reds [Achievement motivators] and the bottom three are the greens [Relationship motivators] ... for me the Motivational Maps really tick the box. With other personality tools I've used in the past it has taken a lot of time to understand what they actually mean. With Motivational Maps you get it straight away and so can move straight onto doing something about it.

At a team level, one of the most positively motivated within the Commercial directorate was the Consultancy and Technical Services team (team motivation at 69% initially and 73% at the time of follow-up). Carl St John Wilson, manager of this team, reports how the maps confirmed and furthered insights about the team to enable actions to meet their motivators further:

> *He was already good at managing his team and we rebalanced things a little to give him even more people management responsibility (for a manager with a high Director motivator whose motivation had improved by 18%).*

> *We carried on more flexible and home working, gave him some better technology to support this, and gave him responsibility for problem solving on some of our really high-priority customers (for a team member high in Searcher and Spirit whose motivation had improved by 36%).*

> *We gave him a group of people to mentor with the challenge of making them as good as he is. At this time he also made it to a more senior position (for a team member with a high Expert and high Builder whose motivation had improved by 10%).*

From a marketing perspective one of the most positive teams was the Press team, led by Rob Andrews. Here motivation increased from 59% to 73%. Rob comments:

> *I strongly believe that the positive change within the team is as a result of the tactics implemented following the Motivational Map training. The results allowed me to develop targeted interventions which met the needs of both the wider team and individuals.*

> *I was pleased to see the results of the team improve following the second survey, and strongly feel that this is down to working on a number of 'little things' rather than one single tactic. The reward strategies provided by James helped me develop a series of measures which were tailored to the team's profile.*

> *From implementing a team mission to away days on the crazy golf course, all of the strategies were well received. The challenge is to keep the positive momentum going, and I am currently looking into strategies to raise the team's profile and recognition across OS.*

Of course, not all motivation levels improved, but in many cases where motivations decreased the Motivational Maps seemed to provide an accurate reflection or helped give a handle on the drop in motivation for the individual:

I think my motivation plummeted due to my Defender. I heard a big announcement that impacted my future, and my Defender needs just shot through the roof. I need to feel secure and have stability, and that just threw everything into question. (A manager with a high Defender in his profile whose motivation dropped by 12%.)

Well this was a year in transition for me. I have done the year and it was a great challenge for me at the time, but now I'm bored and want to be running the show ... my Director motivator wasn't so important before but now I've got my confidence back it is and it's not being met (A senior manager with a high Director in her profile whose motivation dropped by 18%)

In summary, the Motivational Maps have created a welcome buzz and a sense of shared learning across the whole of two business groups. They have given people and their managers some tools to start to work on their motivation levels and have enabled some really empowering conversations for us at OS that are starting to show results.

WHAT NEXT?

We have established a language and shared understanding of Motivational Maps across the two business groups and have enabled some great conversations. The management teams have engaged really well with the Motivational Maps approach,, and we have seen some great case studies where Maps have made a real difference for individuals. We now need to work with our managers and the data we have to enable the best levels of coaching, guidance, and other actions around the Maps to really start to drive motivation across both groups, and ultimately try to tap into that motivation to also drive great performance.

Commentary

'Empowering conversations', 'a language and shared understanding', 'great conversations', 'teams have engaged really well', 'a real difference': these are the phrases being used, which may not sound much initially, but we need to keep in mind that motivation drives performance, which drives productivity, which leads to profit or value if sustained. What is most noteworthy about this case study, so far, is that whilst there is plenty of evidence for improved motivation and performance in certain individuals and teams, even where there has been a drop, the Map language has enabled the employee to understand why and then begin taking remedial action. This is a crucial point, as is the point that just as the increase in motivation cannot be attributed solely to using the Motivational Maps, so neither can the drops: organisations go through a complex series of changes which in themselves can have enormous impacts on the motivations of employees. The key thing the Motivational Maps are supplying is the ability to track what is happening in real time and then to be able to respond to it.

Thus, while the organisation is using Motivational Maps to help two major sections work and communicate more effectively, and in doing so is almost certainly bound to trigger demotivation in those especially who have Relationship-type motivators (and so are change-averse), at the same time the new language is helping those very same people cope – thrive even – with the change because they begin to understand themselves better. One often overlooked fact here is that motivation is not fixed or fatal: it can be changed and we can change our own motivational level (or PMA score). In the work at Ordnance Survey, therefore, the training that was undertaken consistently stressed the fact to employees that whilst they could and should expect their managers to motivate them, they too had a responsibility to motivate themselves. What were they doing about it? What was their action plan to motivate themselves? It was analogous to working out at the gym to improve one's physical condition; working on your own motivation was improving one's emotional state. And one other great thing about this, of course, is that the Motivational Maps are objective and unbiased; in a way the results are simply reflecting back to employees the information that they are inputting. This is not being done to employees, but they are doing it for themselves.

Our next case study was undertaken by one of Motivational Maps' leading business consultants, Susannah Brade-Waring, the Managing Director of Aspirin Business Solutions. Anyone who is a coach, consultant, trainer, HR or organisational development (OD) specialist, or simply a manager, can be trained to understand and deploy this technology. Susannah used Maps with her client, the well-known UK organisation the John Lewis Partnership. Like Ordnance Survey this is an organisation which is highly ethical, people-centric, and value driven, and so the whole ethos of Motivational Maps appeals to them: one key aspect of which is that Maps cannot be a 'top-down' approach, since motivation cannot work like that; it has to be 'bottom-up', which is empowering and also much more effective and long-lasting.

Susannah herself was asked the question, 'How do you improve performance at the John Lewis Partnership?' Her answer was: Motivational Maps! Here is her account of her work with them.

Motivational Maps at the John Lewis Partnership

John Lewis is the UK's largest department store retailer and part of the John Lewis Partnership (JLP). As an organisation, JLP is well respected for its combination of commercial acumen and corporate conscience. It is known for its policy of 'Never Knowingly Undersold', which has been in use since 1925, and for being owned by its employees.

All 93,800 permanent employees are Partners. Together they own 43 John Lewis shops, 337 Waitrose supermarkets, an online and catalogue business, a production unit, and a farm. The business has annual gross sales of over £10bn. The Partners share in the benefits and profits of a business that is based on its founder's vision of a successful business powered by its people and its principles.

Figure 9.3   John Lewis and Waitrose employees

WHY MOTIVATIONAL MAPS?

We started to use Motivational Maps in 2010 in the John Lewis Maintenance department (around 400 Partners). At that time, John Lewis was embarking on a significant expansion of its estate, starting with the first of a new format of stores – John Lewis at Home. These would be stand-alone buildings on retail estates, with a selected product offering which require less floor area and do not need a full complement of staff (Partners). As such they represented a significant change in the Partnership's strategy. In addition, waste and energy initiatives were being introduced, which further increased the scope of the Maintenance Department's service provision.

Like most organisations, JLP wanted to grow whilst maintaining their profit margins. This would require maintaining the headcount, by minimising recruitment and redeploying existing Partners to new roles, and not replacing all retiring Partners etc. However, the Maintenance Department was experiencing a number of challenges, including:

- The Partner Opinion Survey scores for the department were disappointing, particularly around job security. (We subsequently found Defender to be a key motivator of this department, i.e. the need for security, certainty, and predictability.)

- The department was struggling to delegate the waste and energy initiatives, at least partially because the Partners were concerned about providing a reduced service to customers. The lack of capacity for delegation generated real concern about the department's ability to successfully manage the expanding estates without increasing headcount.

Rodney Hoper, Manager of Maintenance at John Lewis (at that time), engaged Aspirin Business Solutions to help the department. His remit:

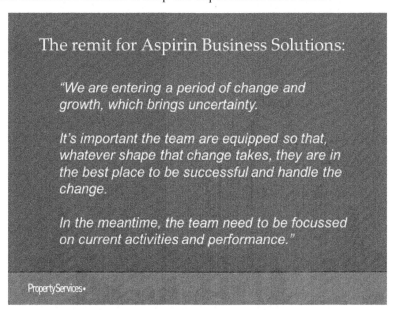

The remit for Aspirin Business Solutions:

"We are entering a period of change and growth, which brings uncertainty.

It's important the team are equipped so that, whatever shape that change takes, they are in the best place to be successful and handle the change.

In the meantime, the team need to be focussed on current activities and performance."

PropertyServices•

Figure 9.4   John Lewis Operations Maintenance remit

Rodney Hoper believed Motivational Maps would help engage the team in embracing the changes through the new strategy, and would provide an essential people-centric element to its annual Maintenance Conference. The conference provided a good opportunity to consult the department about the proposed new vision, strategy, and how performance would be measured.

Rodney particularly liked the Motivational Maps' capability to generate metrics around each individual and each team's level and source of motivation, and the personalised individual reports with motivation strategies.

Figure 9.5   John Lewis Managers for Maintenance with Susannah Brade-Waring

WHAT DID WE DO WITH THE MOTIVATIONAL MAPS?

Susannah Brade-Waring worked with the Operations Managers (OMMs) to map the motivators of the Management Team. The programme started with high-level insights and developed over a number of years into Leadership Coaching for each Operation Manager and their successors.

Phase I   Each OMM completed a Motivational Map and received personalised feedback. This gave them confidence in recommending the tool to their teams.
All 40 Branch Maintenance Managers (BMMs) completed a Motivational Map prior to attending the conference.
At the conference we explored the role of motivation in influencing behaviour, performance, and relationships. We provided an overview of Motivational Maps and then revealed the top three motivators of the team and the lowest motivator.

Phase 1 (cont.)	All attendees were involved in discussions and exercises around these four motivators. This empowered them with knowledge of how their motivation influences their behaviours and choices, and how to manage and feed their motivation.
Phase 2	The OMMs wanted to understand their teams better, and we used the Team Maps to understand the motivators of each regional team. We provided the OMMs with insights specific to their overall team of BMMs and for the individuals. We considered developmental needs and team dynamics. We identified top and 'worst' performers and looked for trends in motivators to explain and predict this. We considered the implications of potential successors and movements of BMMs between the four regions and changes in OMM dynamics (following personnel changes).
Phase 3	Susannah was asked to provide Leadership Coaching to one of the OMMs. The Motivational Map was key to self-awareness, and particularly to identifying and removing blocks or barriers to the individual's progress which were frustrating both the individual and succession planning. As a result, the individual became far more effective at challenging his team's performance and keen to take on more responsibility.
Phase 4	Susannah was asked over the following four years (2011 to date) to provide further Leadership Coaching with Motivational Maps to the other Operations Managers and their successors.
Phase 5	The Leadership and Development Department of John Lewis adopted Motivational Maps as a core tool, and 16 Partners were trained and accredited to use them by a team of Motivational Mappers.

The 2014/15 vision developed by the John Lewis Maintenance Department:

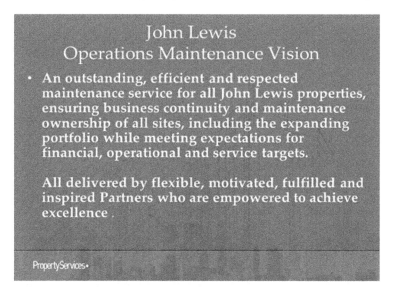

Figure 9.6   John Lewis Operations maintenance vision

HOW DID PEOPLE REACT TO THE MOTIVATIONAL MAPS?

At an individual level the BMMs and OMMs found the Motivational Map questionnaire quick and easy to complete. The speed and online access meant time away from their jobs was kept to a minimum.

The BMMs were given their Motivational Map reports at the end of day one of the conference – after getting insights into their motivation. Many reported staying up late or getting up early to read their Motivational Map report, and found it very interesting and easy to understand:

> *I found the Motivational Map a really interesting and useful exercise, and I think the Maintenance Team will both enjoy and benefit from it.*

> *By understanding my motivators and setting clear expectations, I am far more effective in delivering both personal and business objectives. The Team Map helped us understand each other much better.*

BMMs – Your Team Map

1	SEARCHER		Customer focussed, mission-critical tasks, good causes, seeks meaning, simple, sincere specific feedback
2	DEFENDER		Prudent, consistent, dependable, will stay on track seeks security, predictability, stability
3	SPIRIT		Self driven, focussed, self-sufficient, self-manager seeks freedom, independence, making own decisions
L	STAR		The need to be admired & respected because of one's position is an alien concept, hierarchy has little attraction

How motivated are you as a Team? 73 %

This indicates you are in the 'Boost' zone and are generally well motivated. As a Team, it's likely you perform very well.

You are 54% open to change, as a team.

Figure 9.7   John Lewis Operations Maintenance Team scores

WHAT WAS THE IMPACT OF THE MOTIVATIONAL MAPS?

The first tangible impact was the buzz at the Maintenance Conference. These events tend to be detailed and technical, and the participants showed a much higher level of engagement at a personal level than usual. Feedback following the conference was also positive.

The changes and new strategy were adopted and implemented easily within the team. The team has remained committed to the new strategy and its evolution over the following years. Communication strategies, identified during the conference as part of the Motivational Map exercise, were adopted and supported these changes.

Reflecting back in 2015 at the work we have done with the Maintenance Department of John Lewis we can provide the following update:

In 2010, when we started working with them, the department contained around 400 Partners. This included:

5 OMMs

24 Branch Maintenance Managers

looking after 24 branches and ancillary buildings.

In 2015, the department has:

4 OMMs

23 Branch Maintenance Managers

looking after 43 branches and ancillary buildings (80 buildings in total) – Figure 9.8.

The project has been a commercial success. To date, the increase in productivity has saved the department in the region of £500,000 via saved salary and associated employment costs.

Critically, and in line with the Partnership's principles, the project has also been a success for both customers and Partners, with performance across all areas of the department (Customer, Finance, Operations, and Partner) improving.

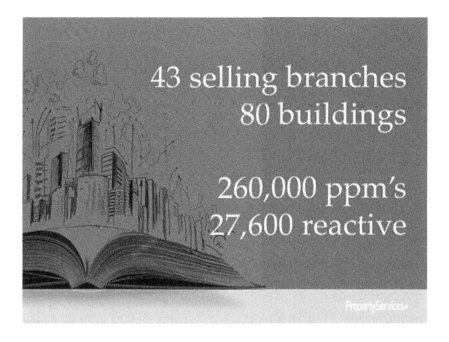

Figure 9.8   John Lewis Maintenance scope of responsibilities

"Susannah's work has been fundamental to our
success in improving a number of areas:

• particularly our Partner and Customer survey
  scores, and

• in creating the highest level of Partner ownership
  I have seen in the department. "

                                    Rodney Hoper, Manager Maintenance

Figure 9.9   Rodney Hoper testimonial

Somewhat surprisingly, the project also increased Partner ownership, particularly as the Partnership is employee owned. We attribute this to the approach applied to this project – that of engaging the department in defining the vision and strategy, ensuring they are motivating, and breaking down the strategy into the measurable factors. This ensured that the Partners were able to measure their own progress and address shortfalls. As the reporting was implemented for every Branch Maintenance Manager, the department is able to benchmark performance across its estate – which has created healthy competition and a way to identify and share areas of best practice.

This sustainable growth and success has been achieved despite fundamental changes in key personnel:

- Rodney Hoper, Manager of Maintenance, retired in 2012 and was succeeded by an experienced Partner who was new to the department.

- Three of the four OMMs have been on their long leave (seven months of paid leave each).

- Their successors (BMMs) have stepped up and not only covered their regions, but also continued to drive improvements in both operational and personal development.

We believe there are three factors which have led to this continued success, despite changes in key personnel:

1. the change management process which ensured that the department was engaged in developing the strategy;

2. the key performance indicators, reporting systems, and continuous improvement; and

3. the Motivational Maps used to create lasting change in people.

The department is currently under review and further expansion of a dozen more branches is planned. Yet I'm advised the mood is positive and the team feel strong. They are indeed 'well equipped so that, whatever shape that change takes, they are in the best place to be successful and handle the change'.

In summary, the Motivational Maps have been fundamental in creating long-lasting and significant changes in attitude and behaviour. The OMMs and BMMs have created more control over their attitude, behaviour, strategy, and how they approach their roles. As a result they feel strong, optimistic, and empowered.

WHAT NEXT?

We are currently using Motivational Maps for Leadership Coaching in the Central Team – which provides specialist technical guidance to the Maintenance Departments of both John Lewis and Waitrose. Long-lasting and remarkable results have been achieved, especially in long-serving Partners who've been with John Lewis for over 20 years.

We have also been engaged to provide Strategic and Leadership Coaching to the Maintenance Department of Waitrose. Starting in April 2015, we will be mapping the motivators of the Management Team – including the Manager of Maintenance, four OMMs and 16 BMMs).

Summary

A number of points should be clear from this case study. First, that motivation and engagement are not some quick fix, not some fad for today, but ongoing issues that need to be worked on. Furthermore, the Motivational Maps are part of the real solution; they provide an invaluable tool as well as a profound source of knowledge and insight into the employees and the teams. But let's not lose sight of the commitment and persistence both of the management itself and of Aspirin Business Solutions, the consultancy they chose to work with them on this. It is dedicated application that gets results, and now those results extend into a fifth year of progress. Also note how not everything is clear or appropriate at the outset: the programme and the process itself lead to exciting new discoveries: in this case, for example, the need for a leadership coaching programme to supplement the other activities. And this programme too is informed by Motivational Maps, for these provide the ideal starting point for a leadership programme, not only from the coaching perspective but also from the leadership model – the '4+1' – we discussed in Chapter 8.

Finally, then, Motivational Maps is the tool par excellence that works with employees and managers to improve performance and productivity, and it does so by non-stereotyping and working with the grain of people. It does not offer a simplistic panacea – take the pill and you will be cured – but rather engages everyone to participate in the development of their own motivations so that they have more energy and focus and satisfaction from their work. Motivational Maps operates exactly where achievement and success are found: the zone of high energy, enthusiasm, and engagement. For that reason alone it will become the tool of choice in the twenty-first century for all discriminating organisations who wish to effect real change and outperform their competitors.

Note

[1] Ordnance Survey was founded in 1746, the year after the final Jacobite Rebellion, and the John Lewis Partnership was founded originally in 1864 when the first shop was opened.

Conclusions

We are now nearing the end of our journey together and I hope you have found this as fascinating, intriguing, and useful as I did when I embarked on the journey well over 10 years ago. Frankly, I had no idea back then just how much was involved in motivation, what areas motivation affected and influenced, and how important motivation is to our organisational prosperity and success, as well as to our own lives.

What have we learnt, then? In the spirit of the Summaries at the end of the first eight chapters, what key nine points are there to emphasise for you?

1. That motivation is an energy that has nine directions or nine faces if you will; and that this energy needs to be seriously focused on if it is going to be harnessed towards high-level performance and organisational achievement.

2. That motivation itself derives from three elements in the human psyche: our personality, our self-concept, and our expectations; and that Motivational Maps reflects this tripartite structure from the manner of its construction.

3. That using Motivational Maps not only provides well over 1 million possible motivational profiles, but also information about our motivations; our attitudes to risk, change, and speed; our preference for Feel, Think, and Know; and our potential Achilles heel of low motivators.

4. There are three good ways to determine your motivators, but the most accurate is the Motivational Map, and this tool also provides Reward Strategy ideas to enable individuals (and teams and organisations) to improve their motivational scores.

5. That motivation has three core personal benefits – energy, enthusiasm, and engagement – and three core organisational

benefits: performance, productivity, and, if the strategy is aligned correctly, profitability.

6.   That motivation underpins highly effective teams and that Motivational Maps can provide amazing insights and support in the building of strong and effective teams.

7.   That the traditionally problematic implementation of Performance Appraisal programmes can be radically reframed and improved using Motivational Maps, and this is by substituting a 'Think' mode approach in the appraisal interview with 'Feel' mode via the Maps.

8.   That probably some 50% at least of both leadership and engagement capabilities stem from motivation and the ability to be able to motivate; and that any attempt to lead or engage without motivation is doomed in the long term.

9.   That leading public sector and commercial organisations in the UK – Ordnance Survey and the John Lewis Partnership – are using this Motivational Maps tool to significant effect in terms of change management, communication, and enabling managers and leaders to more effectively bring employees on board and increase their productivity.

It need hardly be said, of course, on Point 9 that the UK is now only one of 13 countries where the Motivational Maps are being used and the questionnaire online is in a total of six, soon to be seven, languages. There are many other case studies from organisations large and small, public and private sector, commercial and not for profit. And why expect anything else? Motivation is relevant, as we have established, to every organisation and every team and every person because it is about the energy that we need to move us from A, where we are now, to B, where we want to be.

If I may end, then, on a personal note about my journey – a confession if you will – it would be this. When I started this journey it was very much as a business decision: I wanted to run a successful business that focused on motivation. That seemed a natural follow-on from the 10-year management training I had done previously. For any business to survive, let alone succeed, it has to make a profit. In the early days that was very difficult; not so much because we did not have clients who wanted to purchase the Motivational Maps, but because the costs of setting up the structure were so high. But we (my wife and fellow shareholders) persevered because we believed in it and were simply determined whatever the cost to bring Motivational Maps to the world.

Now that has happened, and alongside it an extraordinary extra thing too: the mission has really changed and my own personal mission as well. It's as if 'motivation' has infected everything we do! Sometimes I am asked, 'James, that was a great talk or speech or training session that you did, you were so motivated or you were so energised, but tell me what are you really like?' I guess we all see so many people performing that we suspect a mask; that if we were to catch them off-stage the motivation and the energy simply wouldn't be there. But the truth is: yes, I am always like I am – motivated. Of course, like everybody else, I have my off-moments, but by and large I am fully motivated all the time. This is largely because I know my motivational profile and I feed it – I reward myself continually with small rewards that keep my energy levels up.

The ultimate proof of this came in 2011, five years after I had founded Motivational Maps, when I mysteriously and suddenly fell ill and found myself in the Royal Bournemouth Hospital for three months. I had cancer and I nearly died there, twice. But what amazed, I think, the doctors and the nurses who attended me was my motivation: to live, to get out, and to get back to life. I felt empowered even when I was nearly dead and didn't know whether I actually would live. Of course motivation was not the only factor saving my life: prayer, the love of my wife and family and friends, the skill and care of the doctors and nurses, too; but the strength of my personal motivation was there and I was feeding it internally, strengthening myself and building my energy up, and along with it my hope as well.

Thus I now have a new mission statement in which motivation is central:

> *The focus of my life is to motivate others; it starts with ensuring that I am motivated myself at all times. It extends to my family, friends, and the groups I come into contact with. And my work is to increase people's motivation throughout the world by creating processes, systems, ideas that others can use, enjoy, and develop to their own great advantage. To become so motivated I am enthused in its original meaning: 'godbreathed'.*

From this mission statement of my own, it should come as no surprise that the mission of Motivational Maps Ltd has also changed. Yes, we started out as business trying to add value and make a difference in a local kind of way, but we have now seen the results of our work in so many situations: the profound changes, the deep conversations, the a-ha moments just keep multiplying for us as more and more people, teams, and organisations report back on what has happened as a result of using Maps with their employees, their coaches, and their teams.

We are on a mission now to change how management works throughout the world because we realise that Motivational Maps, as we mentioned before and as I'd like to dwell on in conclusion, is a bottom-up tool: you cannot tell people or managers to be motivated! Using Motivational Maps always presupposes that you are thinking about what to do to engage your employees from their perspective, not yours. Imagine that: their perspective – what do they want? – what floats their boat? – how can I support them by understanding them? By framing it in this way it becomes all too clear that Motivational Maps cannot work any other way, although that will not stop unscrupulous managers wanting to use it to manipulate their employees – something we need to avoid where we find that scenario unfolding. Truly, then, Maps is the friend of the employee and the organisation as it seeks to address the concerns – the desires of both.

But the corollary is this: how big a market is there for Maps? I believe that the Pareto Principle can be invoked here too, for the final time in this book. For most individuals and organisations work is business as usual, is Not Invented Here syndrome, is maximisation of profits at the expense of employees and of everybody and everything else – in short, naked greed and complacency. For these people the idea of imagining what their employees want and going some way towards fulfilling it is unimaginable, an experience beyond which they cannot conceptualise: where's the money in that, they'll ask, despite all the case studies demonstrating the value, and the longer-term returns. We can try to chip away, but a man persuaded against his will, in reality, remains unpersuaded still. No, we need to look for those organisations and people who are visionaries, who are ethical, who empathise and feel compassion for others, and who can really run with Motivational Maps and make the real difference that this tool is capable of delivering for them. How many organisations and people are in this category?

I would guess approximately 20% worldwide. That's right, 1-in-5 of organizations and people in the field worldwide are just waiting to embrace this tool – and suddenly discover the invisible emotions that they can now see and support across their whole organization. And these 1-in-5 will be the drivers and role models for the profound changes that we want in how we work in the future. 1-in-5 of the worldwide total is a pretty enormous and influential number!

It's waiting to happen and I sincerely hope that you, the Reader, having read this book, will want to be part of this motivational movement and join us.

Resources Section

This section of the book is designed to help you find more information about motivation, Motivational Maps, and various organisations and people associated and involved with this project. It is not comprehensive and will doubtless be updated in subsequent editions of the book.

Information about Motivation Maps Ltd and Motivational Maps

Motivational Maps Ltd was founded in 2006. Its product, the Motivational Map, is ISO accredited: ISO 17065; http://www.irqao.org/PDF/C11364-31620.pdf.

The company website can be found at http://www.motivationalmaps.com and enquiries should be addressed to info@motivationalmaps.com.

James Sale, the author, can be found at http://www.jamessale.co.uk and his LinkedIn profile is https://uk.linkedin.com/in/jamesmotivationsale.

There are currently four different Motivational Maps available, although this book covers mainly just one of them, the Motivational Map.

1.   The Motivational Map is for individuals and employees to discover what motivates them and how motivated they are; this produces a 15-page report on the individual.

2.   The Motivational Team Map, which is discussed in Chapter 6. This is a 22+ page report which synthesises the individual Maps from any number of people, and reveals what the overall motivational scores are. It is ideal for team leaders and managers.

3.   The Motivational Organisational Map produces a 36+ page report and synthesises the information from any number of team maps, be they from the whole organisation or a section of the whole organisation. Ideal for senior managers to understand how to implement their strategies through people.

4.   The Motivational Youth Map is different from the other Maps in that it has three outputs – one for the student, one for the teacher, and one for the parent – all designed to help motivate the student to succeed at school and college. Ideal for 11–18-year-olds and school and colleges looking to motivate their students.

The Motivational Map questionnaire is in seven languages: English, German, French, Italian, Greek, Lithuanian, and Portuguese.

Information about Practitioners and Champions of Motivational Maps

Motivational Maps Ltd has trained dozens of consultants, coaches, and trainers to deliver the Maps product as part of a solution offering. Here are some of our key people (UK unless stated otherwise):

PRACTITIONERS

Susannah Brade-Waring, Aspirin Business Solutions, http://www.aspirinbusiness.com – Dorset

Lynne Bell and Kate Turner, Motivational Leadership, http://www.motivationalleadership.co.uk –Wiltshire

Jane Thomas, Premier Life Skills, http://www.premierlifeskills.co.uk – Dorset

Alex Hicks, Motivational Mango Ltd, http://www.momango.biz – Midlands

Roy Duffy, Impact Corporate Development, https://www.linkedin.com/pub/roy-duffy/3/7b8/823 – Somerset

Bevis Moynan, Magenta Coaching Solutions, http://www.magentacs.co.uk – Cambridgeshire

Mark Turner and David Livsey, http://www.motivationalmapseducation.com – Midlands/Yorkshire

Steve Jones, Skills for Business, http://www.skillsforbusinesstraining.co.uk – Hampshire

Akeela Davis, Motivation Maps Solutions, http://motivationmapsolutions. com – Canada

Sylvie Carter, Mindscious, http://www.mindscious.com – Australia

Dorota Raniszewska, Garden HR, http://obrazwcoachingu.pl – Poland

Isaac Peter, People Performance, http://www.ppl-performance.com – Malaysia and Singapore

Morag McGill, Motus Mentis, http://www.motusmentis.it – Italy

Dr Ivo Mersiowsky, http://www.quiridium.de/ – Germany

Julie Schladitz, http://www.sc-careertransition.com/about-us/ – Switzerland

Marie Lucchini, http://www.coach-executives.com/ – Thailand

Tricia Jones, http://www.capacitybuilder.co.za/ – South Africa

CHAMPIONS

Victor Tardieu, Full Circle Motivation, http://www.fullcirclemotivation.com – London

James Watson, Peritus IT Consulting, http://www.watsonsoftware. co.uk – Hampshire

Stephen Feltham, Business Assessment Service, http://www.basltd.co.uk – Dorset

Hugh Liddle, Redcap Sales Coaching, http://www.redcapsalescoaching.com – Florida, USA

James Sale and James on YouTube

More information and videos on James Sale can be found on his personal website: http://www.jamessale.co.uk. James can be found discussing value, energy, and motivation with Jeremy Jacobs on YouTube:

https://www.youtube.com/watch?v=-ScL0jZZC6g

https://www.youtube.com/watch?v=PhgO6DoupWg

https://www.youtube.com/watch?v=wzxQUdH2ExY

https://www.youtube.com/channel/UCZM9oo8Rr0y0byIrJ8gOGXw

Other Key Books on Motivation

Nine books I like on motivation and related topics, but all very different: from being very theoretical and academic to being very readable and practical. See what you think.

Dibley, John, *Let's Get Motivated*, Sidney: Learning Performance, 1992

Francis, Dave, *Managing Your Own Career*, London: Fontana, 1985

Goldberg, Michael J., *9 Ways of Working: How to Use the Enneagram to Discover Your Natural Strengths and Work More Effectively*, New York: Marlowe, 1999

Higgins, E. Tory, *Beyond Pleasure and Pain: How Motivation Works*, Oxford: Oxford University Press, 2014

Lindenfield, Gael, *Self-Motivation*, London: Thorsons, 1996

Miller, William R. and Stephen Rollnick, *Motivational Interviewing: Preparing People for Change*, New York: Guilford, 2002

Persaud, Raj, *The Motivated Mind*, London: Bantam, 2005

Pink, Daniel, *Drive: The Surprising Truth about What Motivates Us*, Edinburgh: Canongate, 2010

Schein, Edgar H., *Career Anchors*, San Francisco: Jossey-Bass, 1990

Three More Books by James Sale

Growing Leaders, Westley: Courseware, 1998.

York Notes: Macbeth, London: Longman, 1997, 2002, 2010.

Inside the Whale, [n.p.]: Lulu, 2012.

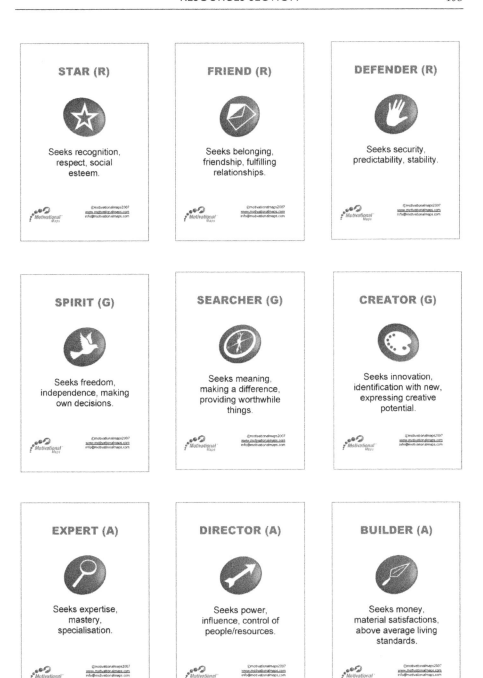

Figure R.1   Nine cards for motivation card game

DEFENDER		*Stable and secure organisation; Predictable advancement within organisation; Routine/repetitive work*
FRIEND		*Strong team ethos; Excellent social & "extra-curricular" activities; caring management*
STAR		*Clear job titles, visible recognition; Hierarchical structure; Perks linked to level within organisation*
DIRECTOR		*Responsibility built into role; Clear promotion and/or career prospects; Control of resources*
BUILDER		*Performance and reward clearly linked; Commission, bonuses; Above average rates of pay*
EXPERT		*Technical positions; Professional environments; High skill and/or knowledge jobs*
CREATOR		*Problem-solving/developmental work; High change/challenge Environments; Stream of new initiatives*
SPIRIT		*Lack of close supervision; Ability to make own decisions/discretion; Can prioritise own time*
SEARCHER		*Voluntary Sector/Charity; Customer-facing role; Mission-critical tasks/projects*

Figure R.2   Motivational Map career choices

MONEY tangible	How much: From where:	
TIME intangible	When: How much:	
EQUIPMENT tangible	What: Where from:	
PEOPLE SKILLS People development	Which: Level:	
KNOWLEDGE intangible	What: Level:	
RIGHT ATTITUDE People development	Approach: Motivation:	
INFORMATION intangible	What: Format:	
SPACE/ENVIRONMENT tangible	Where: Quality:	
AGREE CO-OPERATION People development	Who: When:	

Figure R.3   Nine kinds of resources for change

Index

Made in the USA
Monee, IL
21 January 2022

89450873R10125